THE KORSTEN BASKETMAKERS

To my parents

THE KORSTEN BASKETMAKERS

A STUDY OF THE MASOWE APOSTLES, AN INDIGENOUS AFRICAN RELIGIOUS MOVEMENT

by

CLIVE M. DILLON-MALONE, S.J.

Published for
THE INSTITUTE FOR AFRICAN STUDIES
UNIVERSITY OF ZAMBIA
by
MANCHESTER UNIVERSITY PRESS

© INSTITUTE FOR AFRICAN STUDIES, UNIVERSITY OF ZAMBIA, 1978

Published on behalf of
THE INSTITUTE FOR AFRICAN STUDIES
UNIVERSITY OF ZAMBIA
P.O. Box 900, Lusaka

by

MANCHESTER UNIVERSITY PRESS
Oxford Road, Manchester M13 9PL

Cased edition distributed in the U.S.A. by

HUMANITIES PRESS INC.

Atlantic Highlands, N.J. 07716

British Library Cataloguing in Publication Data

Dillon-Malone, Clive Mary
    The Korsten basketmakers.
    1. Masowe Apostles
    I. Title. II. University of Zambia. Institute for African Studies
    289.8   BX9998.M/

    ISBN 0–7190–1042–X (cased)
    ISBN 0–7190–1410–7 (Zambian Paper)

Printed in Great Britain at The Pitman Press, Bath

CONTENTS

v

LIST OF ILLUSTRATIONS

AUTHOR'S NOTE

The present work is based on a doctoral thesis which was presented to Fordham University, New York, in February, 1976. The thesis itself contains numerous appendices, including an historical account of the Masowe Apostles as narrated by evangelist Cyprian Nedewedzo, a selection of materials collected during personal interviews and Masowe prayer services, and a brief account of methodology and research techniques used. Most of the appendices have had to be omitted here.

This study was carried out under very difficult circumstances and the nature of the treatment given to the material which follows bears the clear marks of numerous limitations. When I began to carry out research among the Masowe Apostles in Zambia in October 1973, I was wholly unaware of the fact that Johane Masowe, the founder of this religious movement, had just recently died in Zambia and that his remains had been flown to Rhodesia for burial. Even more serious was the fact that a widespread split which had taken place among the Apostles on the occasion of the death of the founder had escaped my attention. Hence, my appearance on the scene among the Apostles was greeted with much caution and suspicion. Added to this was the fact that I had been unwittingly attempting to establish contact with members of both the splinter group and the main group, an action which had rendered me all the more unacceptable to both groups. When I finally did manage to gain a measure of acceptance among the main group, my contacts were of necessity restricted to the leaders and the elders. For these reasons, sociological data of the more quantitative type was not possible to obtain on a wide scale.

What follows, then, focuses strongly on an attempt to understand the motivating power of religious belief on an indigenous African religious movement and its effect on the religious ritual and way of life of its members. This study is very much in the nature of a pioneering work and it is hoped that it will stimulate further research of a more detailed and quantitative nature on particular Masowe communities.

FOREWORD

Since the early nineteen-sixties political events in south central Africa have tended to monopolise the public attention, although in this context the older churches have sometimes figured through an attack on a mission station, the deportation of a bishop, or a statement from church leaders. The new religious movements and independent churches have been much less prominent, although there were the Lumpa Church troubles in Zambia that featured in the world's news headlines for some months in 1964, and the occasional reference to Jehovah's Witnesses as refugees. This area, however, is especially rich in the variety and size of its independent religious movements, and in the number and quality of the studies made of them. The list of major monographs is impressive: R. L. Wishlade on Malawi (1965), Sister Mary Aquina on Rhodesian churches (1966, 1967), M. W. Murphree on the Shona (1969), M.-L. Martin on Mai Chaza's church in Rhodesia (1971), M. L. Daneel's first two volumes on the Southern Shona independents (1971, 1974), and B. Jules-Rosette's study of Johane Maranke's church (1975); add the various writings of T. O. Ranger and his associates on this area, and a number of doctoral dissertations. No area of Africa has been better served for serious work on this theme, and one can only wish that the older churches and missions had been served equally well.

There was, however, still need for a major study of the large and important body variously known as Johane Masowe's Apostles, the Apostolic Sabbath Church of God, the Africa Gospel Church, the Gospel of God Church, or more popularly as the Korsten Basketmakers. Dr. Dillon-Malone has now supplied this and opened up a whole new range of information with a straightforward study of the historical and religious dimensions of this movement. These two emphases are entirely appropriate in a first study, for one senses that the author is writing with the Apostles and for them, enabling them to discover their own history in one single perspective, and so to establish their own identity more clearly. This is a task that has overtaken the historical scholar in various parts of the world and that presents new problems of what to say, how to say it, and what to omit, at least for the present. And since these folk form what is primarily a religious community, and certainly see themselves as such, it is fitting that this aspect should predominate, rather than questions concerning the influence of the traditional culture or of the more recent social, economic and political context. These aspects are not ignored in this work but there is plenty of room for further detailed investigation in these areas.

It is immediately apparent from this study that the Korsten Basketmakers clearly exhibit what might by now be called a classic pattern for such movements. There are the wonders surrounding the birth and infancy of the founder, and the visions and death-with-resurrection experience that constitute his call and charter as a prophet. There is the hostility to traditional religious forms and to

ix

witchcraft and magic, combined with independence from the older churches without loss of an emphasis on the Bible. There is the moral-legalistic form of religion, and the puritan-ascetic ethic, the emphasis upon baptism and the neglect of the Holy Communion, the remarkable missionary dynamic that has taken the movement from the Rhodesia of its origins to eight other African countries, and as the ending of its foundation phase the death of the prophet John Masowe with the consequent succession struggles and schism.

At the same time there are warnings against stereotyping these movements, for this one in particular reveals its own distinctive features and some very un-African forms. Here is a new religious movement without drums or dancing, with no clapping and no other musical instruments, but with a strong emphasis on singing; here are no staffs like so many others around them, and no holy water or other healing medium to support its spiritual healing practice. The establishment of a women's convent of 'sisters' or 'spiritual wives' to serve as guardian and transmitter of the tradition is a most unusual religious form. Also remarkable is the migrant history that has freed the Apostles from the bonds of land and tribe; first near Salisbury then to Bulawayo, on to the Transvaal and then settled for fifteen years near Port Elizabeth at Korsten, deported back to Rhodesia and then spreading to so many other countries and planning to make their headquarters in Nairobi as a base for a moving on to Egypt and Jerusalem. Throughout this Abrahamic existence their unity and identity were preserved. Behind this there has been another kind of migration in progress, a steady shift across the spectrum of what might be called their religious content. Starting from an apparently syncretist position where there was some deliberate synthesis of the new and the old religious worlds, they seem to have moved to what I call a Hebraist position, notably biblical in form but without a christology that would enable them to be described as an independent church.

This shift towards the more orthodox Christian end of the spectrum bears out D. B. Barrett's thesis about the importance of the Scriptures in the rise and history of these movements. By the nineteen-twenties all four of the main peoples in the Shona language group had their own complete translations of the New Testament, and the Bible appears as the central religious object in the Masowe Apostles. The direction of religious change within the movement is all the more remarkable when we learn that it had nativistic, anti-white, somewhat millennial overtones in its earlier stages, and that these emphases were supported by various unorthodox or anti-church religious movements such as the pentecostal Apostolic Faith Mission from South Africa, the millennial Watch Tower or Jehovah's Witnesses, and the nativistic Church of the White Bird. The Apostles have followed none of these local patterns but have created their own distinctive community and identity, with a system of belief that combines much of the old world view with increasing appropriations from the new world of the Bible. In so doing this movement is acting as an effective agent of change for those in transition from the old Africa to the new.

Note should be taken of the valuable appendices providing primary documentation, and readers should be aware that the original dissertation upon which this volume is based contains a much greater assembly of primary sources

as starting points for future researchers, together with an essay on the
methodology and techniques of field research as these worked out in practice for
the author. Dr. Dillon-Malone is aware that his material comes primarily from a
select number of the leaders, and only from the loyalist section after the schism,
and therefore represents a more "official" history and more normative beliefs
than those of the rank and file. He also discovered how the data led him and conditioned the methods he used, and this would seem to be the better procedure in
the first study of such a movement; more deliberate and sophisticated methods
can be used later and by others. All such further research will benefit from this
foundation account of another major African religious movement.

Project for the Study of New   Harold W. Turner
Religious Movements in Primal
Societies, University of Aberdeen

INTRODUCTION

The rapid and widespread growth of new religious movements in Africa since the beginning of the twentieth century has already assumed continental proportions, and Harold Turner (1971, 1–10) has noted that it is now worthy of consideration as a new field in the history of religions. Bengt Sundkler (1964) was the first to bring to the attention of scholars the vast proliferation of prophet movements in South Africa, and David Barrett (1968) followed up with the much more comprehensive analysis of the phenomenon of religious independency for the whole of sub-Saharan Africa. In the latter work, it has been noted that these independent religious movements 'were known to number by 1967 some five thousand distinct ecclesiastical and religious bodies in thirty-four African nations, with a total of almost seven million nominal adherents drawn predominantly from two hundred and ninety different tribes in all parts of the continent' (Barrett, 1968, 3). While much writing of a general nature, however, has appeared in connection with these movements (Mitchell & Turner, 1966; Turner, 1968, 173–211; 1970, 161–208), few major monographical studies have been carried out (Turner, 1967; Peel, 1968). The present work on the Masowe Apostles hopes to narrow that gap.

A wide variety of diverse religious movements outside of Africa has been studied under the heading of 'revitalisation movements' (Wallace, 1956, 264–81), and various forms of millenarianism, nativism and messianism have received dominant emphasis. In the case of the Masowe Apostles, however, any such exaggerated emphasis is lacking, although it will be clear that mild forms of such characteristics have been present particularly in the early stages of their development.[1] In regard to religious movements in the Western world, the sect to church typology has held the field for a very long time. First popularised by Ernest Troeltsch (1931, I: 331–43), and later refined by Richard Niebuhr (1929) who pointed out that sects tend to develop into denominations, more recent studies have shown that sects do, in fact, develop along a variety of different paths (Wilson, 1961; 1967a; 1967b, 303–17; O'Dea, 1957). Sects have been defined as movements of religious protest, and it has been shown that certain sects may continue

[1] See pp. 17–18.

1

to preserve their initial protest within the framework of a more organised institutional structure. Hence, the concept of an established-sect has been introduced. Werner Stark (1967, 306) does not accept the latter concept, but regards the process of 'settling down into abiding forms' as the common denominator in the shift from sect to denomination, a shift from dynamic life and spontaneity to routine and formality. In the terminology of Max Weber (1969, 370) it is the consequence of the routinisation of charisma.

The usefulness of the sect-church typology in regard to religious movements in Africa has been questioned (Peel, 1968, 237), and even in the Western world it has been pointed out that 'probably nowhere in a sociological discourse is essential consensus on meaning of concepts so lacking' (Coleman, 1968, 59). Furthermore, the term 'sect' has taken on strongly derogatory and pejorative connotations which tend to focus on the negative, rather than on the positive, aspects of religious movements. Religious movements in Africa have arisen in situations of culture contact which are very different from those in which religious movements have arisen in the Western world, and there is the danger of drawing too close a parallel between the two.

Numerous typologies have been suggested for religious movements in Africa (Turner, 1967b, 33; Barrett, 1968, 48; Oosthuizen, 1968, 71–73; Fernandez, 1969; 34; Dillon-Malone, 1973, 6). The first and still the most commonly used—although by no means a satisfactory one—is that of Sundkler (1964, 53–59, 302) who distinguished the Ethiopian and the Zionist types (a third Messianic type being a sub-category of the Zionist type). The former type refers to large secession groups from European churches which, in many cases, turn out to be almost carbon copies of the parent churches; the latter type refers to those religious movements which have grown up under the initiative and leadership of some African prophet outside the established mission churches. The Masowe Apostles fall under the Zionist type. At the Mindolo Conference held in Zambia in 1962, the following descriptive definition was put forward:

> Zionist or Aladura Churches are those in which the emphasis is on the work of the holy spirit, with particular reference to various forms of revelation and healing, re-interpreted in terms of the felt needs of the local culture (Hayward, 1963, 71).

Similar movements have also been described as 'pentecostal', 'prayer-healing' and 'prophet-healing' churches (Turner, 1967b, 22). In his study of religious movements in Rhodesia, Martinus Daneel (1971, 5–6, 285–345) has grouped Zionist and Apostolic churches under the heading of 'Spirit-type' churches, and the two Apostolic churches he mentions are the Maranke Apostles and the Masowe Apostles.

It can be seen from the above that African religious movements are commonly referred to as 'churches', not with reference to the sect-church typology, but emphasising rather the fact that they cater fully to the religious needs of their followers. African independent religious movements prefer to be referred to as churches, and at the All African Council of Churches held at Abidjan in September 1969, they voiced their preference for the title 'African Indigenous Churches'. Due to the misleading and confusing implications of the terms 'sect' and 'church', then, I have decided to refer to the religious movement founded by Johane Masowe as the 'Masowe Apostles', or simply as the 'Apostles', in the pages that follow—although they are formally registered as the 'Gospel of God Church'. At the same time, I intend to avail myself of the conceptual framework within which the sect-church typology has been discussed. Particular emphasis will be placed on the migrant nature of the central body of the Masowe Apostles, and on the question of social and religious change in the context of the dialectical interplay between the Apostles and the wider society in the various countries in which they have lived (see chapter VI) (Redekop, 1974, 345–52). In terms of the sect-church typology itself, it could be said, in general, that the Masowe Apostles have developed from the position of a sect to that of an established-sect, for 'the established sect', according to Milton Yinger, 'is somewhat more inclusive, less alienated, and more structured than the sect, and therefore closer to the denomination' (1971, 266–7).

The sociological concepts of 'anomie' (i.e., the breakdown of social norms and structures of authority) and 'relative deprivation' (i.e., an awareness of unfulfilled needs) have been commonly used in regard to the emergence of religious movements, and their use will be seen to be very relevant in the case of the Masowe Apostles as well. Particular emphasis, however, will be placed on the religious visions and the conversion experience of the prophet-founder himself, for as Peel has correctly observed:

> The sociology of a new religion must start off . . . from the religious motivations, the doctrinal pronouncements of the founders, seen as answers to religious problems (1968, 14).

It will be seen that the conscious motivating power which impelled the religious behaviour of Johane and his inner core of disciples was an explicit awareness and conviction of being called by God to perform the work of salvation among African peoples. This notion will be described in terms of the concept of charisma in chapter V. The basic hypothesis of this study is that, in a situation of prolonged culture con-

tact with white Christianity and Western secularisation, a specific segment of Shona society had responded to the Bible at a time of particular stress in a creative manner which was relevant, meaningful and
suited to its own felt needs. A corollary to this hypothesis would be the
keen awareness among certain Africans of the inadequacy of white
Western Christianity to respond to both old and new religious needs in
a satisfactory manner.

Finally, it should be noted that, while effects are very different from
causes, they can often demonstrate the presence of certain implicit and
hidden needs. Such a procedure involves a process of inference, but as
Arthur Stinchcombe has observed, 'it is always a good bet, in trying to
explain a social phenomenon, to look at its consequences' (1968, 99).
On the other hand, it must be remembered that the conditions which
give rise to religious movements may not persist, and religions may
succeed in performing functions for their members not intended by the
founder.

It is important to clarify what this present work deals with and what
it does not deal with. In general, it is a monographical study of an
African indigenous religious movement which began in Southern
Rhodesia in 1932 among the Shona. In particular, however, it deals
with the central group of the Masowe Apostles, viz., that body which
had remained close to the founder right from the start and had
travelled with him. It does not deal with the numerous Masowe communities which have now become established in various parts of
Africa. Johane Masowe died in 1973 so that the present work covers the
complete era in which the founder lived. The history of the Masowe
Apostles has been traced through the central group, and knowledge of
Masowe belief and ritual has been largely the result of contact with the
central group at Marrapodi, Lusaka, Zambia. This means that the
study has focused upon the ideals of the Apostles in a particularly
privileged case. On the other hand, it must be emphasised that,
although other Masowe communities, particularly in the rural areas,
may not correspond in detail to the picture portrayed here, the
strength and purity of a religious movement resides in its central core.
A second reservation needs to be made. A split occurred among the
Apostles on the death of the founder resulting in two groups, viz., the
loyalist and the rebel groups. This study deals only with the loyalist
group.

In the first of a four-volume study of the Southern Shona independent churches in Rhodesia, Martinus Daneel (1971, 339–41) has made
a brief reference to the 'Apostolic Sabbath Church of God of Johane
Masowe (or Gandanzara)' in which he states that he has not particularly studied this movement. I am especially indebted to this work,

however, for the wealth of information which it supplies concerning the general background of religious independency in Rhodesia as well as for its analysis of traditional Shona religion and social structure.

I would like to express my gratitude to the many leaders among the Masowe Apostles with whom I have had lengthy conversations in Rhodesia, Zambia and Kenya. My special thanks are due to evangelist Cyprian Nedewedzo Nhamburo, the present leader of the loyalist Apostles, to pastor Amon Ngomasha, the church secretary at its headquarters in Marrapodi, Lusaka, and to the Sisters in Lusaka and Nairobi. My thanks are also due to the administrative staff of the National Archives of Rhodesia for their kindness and co-operation in helping me to find the material on which so much of the early part of this work depends. Likewise, I wish to thank the staff of the National Archives of Zambia.

For their encouragement, help and direction in the preparation and ordering of the content of this work, I wish to acknowledge my gratitude to Professor Werner Stark, Dr. Charles Serei, S. J., and Dr. James Kelly, all of Fordham University. For financial assistance in the course of my research work, and for making possible the printing and publication of this work, I wish to acknowledge my sincere thanks to MISEREOR, Germany, and MISSIO, Germany, respectively.

Finally, I wish to express my indebtedness to the following who translated Shona material into English for me: Mr Tobias Chawatama (assistant to Rev. Desmond Dale, S. J., at the Shona language laboratory in Salisbury); Mr Weston Chatora (postgraduate student at the University of Zambia); and two Shona Jesuit novices in Lusaka, viz., Rev. Felix Gwanzura and Rev. Philip Kavai Chidyamudungwe.

CHAPTER I

THE APOSTLES OF JOHANE MASOWE

GENERAL BACKGROUND

(i) Socio-Economic. The country of Rhodesia in Africa (formerly Southern Rhodesia) has been divided into the administrative divisions of Mashonaland and Matabeleland. The former is occupied by the Shona Bantu group which, according to the linguistic distribution of Doke (1954, 21), comprises the Korekore, Zezuru, Karanga, Manyika and Ndau; the latter is occupied by the Ndebele-Zulu who invaded Southern Rhodesia in the nineteenth century, but who, in fact, only inhabit the territory surrounding Bulawayo (see map 1). The Kalanga—living around Plumtree but stretching into Botswana—also belong to the Shona group, but they became geographically separated at the time of the Ndebele invasion. The Manyika and Ndau stretch into the territory of Mozambique as well, and the Korekore stretch into both Mozambique and Zambia.

The Shona and Ndebele peoples had joined together in armed uprisings in 1896 and 1897 in an attempt to overthrow their white oppressors, but the attempt had ended in miserable failure (Ranger, 1967, 268–310). Shona religious authorities had, in fact, played a major part in organising the rebellions, and their position had become considerably weakened as a result (Ranger, 1966, 94–136). The outcome of the risings had demonstrated to the Shona the utter futility of seeking for their freedom by military means. By the first decade of the twentieth century, a new sense of optimism had begun to set in with the development of an enterprising rural economy, and a certain degree of independence was experienced. This had all changed, however, by the end of the First World War. As Ranger has observed,

> The rural economy ceased to produce and to market successfully a sizeable agricultural surplus; Shona men were compelled to enter the labour market in ever-increasing numbers, and at a time when wages were low; prices for African produce and stock declined (Ranger, 1970, 194).

Rural-urban mobility had increased on a large scale as African labourers sought for employment in the towns, in the mines or on European farms. The young men especially had begun to spend long periods away from home, only returning at periodic intervals. The big blow to the urban worker, however, had come at the end of the 1920s as the economic depression swept through Southern Rhodesia.

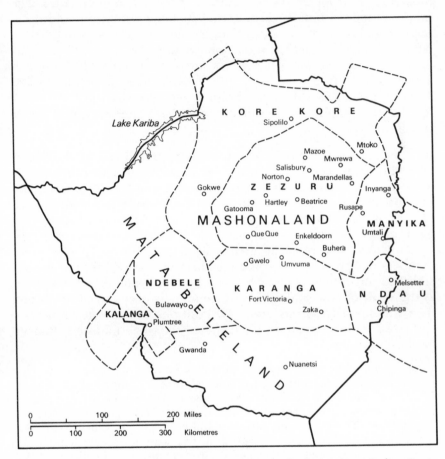

MAP 1. Linguistic distribution of peoples of Rhodesia. (See Doke, *Bantu Languages,* map at end.)

Labourers had suddenly found themselves unemployed and with little or no prospect of earning the cash income on which they had become so dependent. In 1931, Southern Rhodesia's principal export, i.e., tobacco, had dropped to one-eighth of its record output in 1928. The output of gold, asbestos, chrome, and coal had also begun to drop in the mines. The result was such that, by the early 1930s, young Shona labourers were wandering about jobless and idle, and with little interest or incentive to work in the rural areas which offered little hope of a cash return as both maize and cattle had become gluts on the market. The overall situation, then, had become one of frustration and despair for the young Shona, in particular, who had come to expect better things.

(ii) Religious. Christianity had been first introduced among the Shona by a Portuguese Jesuit missionary, Fr Gonzalo de Silveira, in 1561. It was only in 1890, however, when the British South African Company took possession of Southern Rhodesia, that Christian mission bodies had taken firm root there. By 1900, ten different denominations had been presented with Government land grants in Shona territory covering 325,730 acres (Murphree, 1969, 6–7). By the early 1920s great numbers of Shona had become members of one or other of the established mission churches. They had become familiar with the Bible as the word of God and had been continually encouraged to discard their traditional religious practices. Positions of authority, however, had continued to remain in the hands of the white ministers. Ranger has observed that:

> at the end of the 1920s there was still only a handful of African clergy. The two denominations which had progressed furthest in the production of an African ministry were the Anglicans and the Wesleyans. In 1930, there were seven African Anglican priests and twelve African Wesleyan ministers. There were no African Catholic priests or Dutch Reformed Church ministers. The Salvation Army, with its more democratic traditions, possessed as many as sixty-five 'commissioned native officers', but other than these, there were only some two dozen African clergy in Southern Rhodesia (1970, 191–2).

Due to the fact that the white churches had become firmly established at the same time as the white colonial rulers, it is not surprising that many Africans tended to think of them both as being closely connected. Although the Shona, however, had been able to exercise little power in the white world of religion and politics, yet they had gradually come to realise that the Bible could not be controlled exclusively by the white churches, especially when—by the 1920s–the whole of the New Testament had been translated and printed in Karanga, Zezuru,

Manyika and Ndau (Doke, 1954, 205). The literate Shona now had the opportunity, at least, of making an independent response to the contents of the Bible.

During the 1920s the Southern Rhodesian authorities had become very concerned over the inroads which certain European-inspired religious bodies had been making into the country from both the north and the south. Numerous African religious movements had already originated in South Africa under African prophets, many of whom were claiming to be the Black Jesus. Labour migrants from Southern Rhodesia, who had come into contact with these movements, were bringing back similar ideas to their own people. Just as the political slogan of 'Africa for the Africans' was to become a widespread cry, so a similar trend of thought in the form of a black Jesus for the Africans had taken root. One of the movements which had been causing most concern in the early 1930s and which was under white leadership, was the Apostolic Faith Mission Church of South Africa. The AFM had first come into Southern Rhodesia in 1918 under the leadership of one Luttig, a European from South Africa, and one Dingiswayo, a Nyasa preacher, and it had established itself in the Gatooma district of Mashonaland (see map 2). In 1919 the Chief Native Commissioner (CNC) had expressed strong disapproval of its presence and activity as follows:

> Faith-healing and emotionalism are prominent features of this sect. The psychic and moral effect of such teaching, to my mind, must tend to foster delusions among the native community. . . . Emissaries of such sects are a menace to the Administration by stirring up discontent among the natives.[2]

Despite this observation, however, the AFM continued to entrench itself firmly throughout Mashonaland in the 1920s and by 1933 its African preachers were moving about freely under no apparent supervision.

Although the AFM, then, with its pentecostal-type features, was a cause for much concern on the part of the Southern Rhodesian authorities, the influence of the Watch Tower movement from the north with its millennial-type characteristics was an even greater cause for worry. The Watch Tower movement had become very powerful in Nyasaland (now Malawi) at the beginning of the twentieth century under the leadership of Kenan Chirwa Elliot Kamwana, a Tonga from Nyasaland. The explosive potential of Watch Tower teaching had manifested itself soon afterwards under John Chilembwe and Tom

[2] Chief Native Commissioner to Secretary of Administrator, 1919, National Archives of Rhodesia, File S84/A/275 quoted in Daneel, 1967, p. 391.

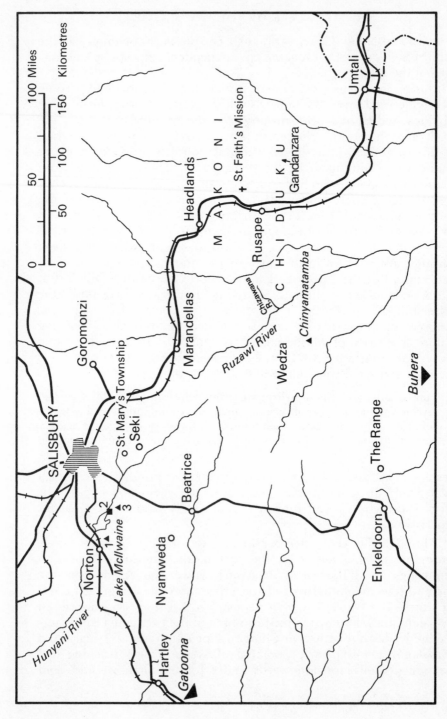

MAP 2. Central Mashonaland, Rhodesia. 1 Marimba Hill, 2 Elladale Farm, 3 Nyamatara Hill.

Nyirenda, the latter of whom was popularly known as 'Mwanalesa' (son of God) (Shepperson & Price, 1958). The Southern Rhodesian Government had for long feared the movement south of Watch Tower, and it became known in the 1920s that a dedicated Watch Tower missionary named Kunga had appeared in Bulawayo (Ranger, 1970, 200). By the end of the 1920s Watch Tower had spread its influence to the rural areas of Mashonaland. The first indigenous African religious movement among the Shona, viz., 'The Church of the White Bird' founded by Matthew Zwimba in 1915, had most probably been influenced by Watch Tower teaching. Ranger notes that 'it was an alien millenarian movement which made no direct appeal back to 1896 and 1897 [i.e., the Shona-Ndebele Risings], but which effectively presented itself as a successor that swept the rural district of Mashonaland in the late 1920s' (Ranger, 1967, 380).

When Southern Rhodesia was granted Responsible Government in 1923, a Bill was drafted with regard to the control of the teaching and conduct of wandering African preachers. The bill was first put before the Missionary Conference (founded in 1903 and to which most Protestant bodies were affiliated) for its approval, and, to the great surprise of the authorities, it was rejected on the grounds of constituting an infringement of religious liberty (Daneel, 1971, 399–400). As a result, the Native Department had 'to continue to deal with Separatist preachers by the same "informal" measures of coercion combined with prosecution under various statutes and proclamations not connected with religious teaching at all which had served it in the past' (Ranger quoted in Daneel, 1971, 40). In 1926 it was suggested that African preachers should not be allowed to function unless they were under the control of some European leader residing in the country, and it was on this point that the authorities had begun to confront them. Legislation, however, had never been passed on the matter.

THE APPEARANCE OF JOHANE MASOWE:
PROPHET AMONG THE SHONA

Towards the end of October 1932 the Chief Native Commissioner (CNC) in Salisbury was informed that an African Prophet—calling himself 'John the Baptist'—was preaching in the Hartley district of central Mashonaland. Apparently, he had succeeded in attracting a large following. Enquiries were immediately set in motion revealing the fact that the prophet's name was Shoniwa and that his registration number was x3026 from the district of chief Makoni.[3] It transpired that

[3] See Registration Card filed at District Commissioner's Office, Rusape, Rhodesia.

Shoniwa had been arrested in February of that year for trespassing at Norton. At that time, he had been travelling under the fictitious name of 'Mtunyane' and had not been in possession of a registration certificate.[4] On 1 November, 1932 Shoniwa was brought before the CNC for questioning—once again, not being in possession of a registration certificate—and he gave the following account of the manner and circumstances of his religious experiences:

> At the early part of this year, I went to Norton and was employed by a native named Jack as a shoemaker, with whom I remained for two months. I left this native as I became sick. I had very severe pains in the head which caused me to lose my speech for four months. I remained in the compound of Mr Maitland's farm. I received medicine (native) from my late employer, Jack. At the time [that] I was suffering from these headaches, I was unable to walk about.
>
> During my sickness, I had a dream one day. I dreamt that I was dead. I heard a voice telling me to pray to God. When I awoke, I prayed to God and lit seven candles that I had in the hut. It was during my illness that I heard voices telling me that I was John. I had never been called that name before. I thought that I was meant to be called 'John the Baptist'. I therefore used that name. I felt that when that name was given to me that I should go and preach to the natives. I think that I was given that name, 'John the Baptist', by God.
>
> Up to the time that I was sick, I studied the Bible that I had continuously, and also when I was sick. The Bible I had, I bought in Salisbury from a shop in Second Street. It was in the native language.
>
> When I got better, I left the compound that I was staying in and went to a hill near Norton and remained there for forty days praying by myself. The only food I had during this time was wild honey. I prayed to heaven day and night. I did not sleep. Whilst staying on the hill, I used to hear a voice saying, 'I have blessed you. Carry on with the good work. Tell the natives to throw away their witchcraft medicines, not to commit adultery or rape....'
>
> I really do believe that I have been sent from heaven to carry out religious work among the natives. I think that I am 'John the Baptist', as the voice told me so. No human being has guided me in my teachings. I am only guided by the voice that I heard when I was staying on the hill for forty days. I have heard the voice since in my dreams. The voice would come to me through a bush that was burning quite near me. When the voice ceased, the fire would go out.
>
> I no longer suffer from pains in the head (A3–5, 10–11).[5]

---

[4] See reference given under File 1 on p. 156 below. The full references to material obtained from the National Archives of Rhodesia are given on pp. 156–7 below and will be referred to for brevity in the text under a single file number.

[5] References to material given in full in appendices A and B will be indicated by a capital letter referring to the appropriate appendix and a number referring to the appropriate section.

The picture which emerges from the account above is that of a profound religious experience expressed in terms of traditional and biblical imagery and resulting in a firm personal conviction of a call from God to perform a special work among Africans. The role which Shoniwa felt himself called to fill, however, was in no way original or unique to himself. Earlier that same year, another Shona prophet by the name of John Maranke had felt himself called to perform a similar role (Nyamwena, n.d.), and John the Baptist had become the standard biblical type of the African prophet (Sundkler, 1964, 208, 277). On the other hand, the manner in which various African prophets have experienced and expressed their call has frequently tended to be creative and unique in particular cases.

It would appear that Shoniwa was most familiar with the Gospels and the Acts of the Apostles, and the title given to the followers of Jesus determined what his own followers should be called. His religious call hinged on three biblical figures, viz., Moses, John the Baptist, and Jesus, although conscious attention was focused upon the figure of John the Baptist. The reference to the voice heard in the burning bush

FIG. 1. Johane Masowe.

was a clear allusion to the call of Moses as described in the Book of Exodus in chapter three, but Shoniwa may have adverted to it more directly in Acts 7:30–34. The mention of forty days spent on a hill in prayer with hardly any food would seem to have alluded to the period spent in the wilderness by Jesus (Mt. 4:2), whereas the reference to honey, as well as the commission to preach to his people to repent of their evil ways, alluded more directly to the figure of John the Baptist. Shoniwa was convinced that his call had come from heaven and not from any human source and, although he did not explicitly mention the name of God, it is clearly Jehovah to whom he was referring.

Shoniwa's religious experience also contained strong traditional features. A prolonged illness of a psychosomatic nature was a traditionally recognised sign of the desire of some spirit to take possession of a human being (Gelfand, 1962, 21; Daneel, 1971, 100, also see 84–5, 91–2). Furthermore, a dream or a vision was traditionally looked upon as a standard mechanism for communication between the spirit world and human beings. The notion of God manifesting himself by speaking in a tree was also a traditional religious concept (Gelfand, 1959, 201). It is most probable that Shoniwa did, in fact, suffer from some kind of illness—an illness which his followers later attributed to a fall from a bicycle (see p. 53 below)—but what is of key importance is the manner in which he himself interpreted its significance. For Shoniwa, it was a clear sign of a call to perform a special religious work among his own people.

Shoniwa Masedza Tandi Moyo, the second eldest of six sons and one daughter born to Jack and Efie Masedza, was himself born at Gandanzara in the Makoni district of central Mashonaland near Rusape (see map 2 on p. 10 above). He was a Mahungwe by tribe (AI) which means that he spoke a dialect of Manyika (Doke, 1954, 22). His parents were members of the Anglican Church in which he himself was baptised as Peter (B17). When he was young, he attended the Anglican Missions of St. Faith and St. Colombus (A2) and he grew up under the care of his uncle, John Mugwambi, who had been a minister in the Wesleyan Methodist Church. Shoniwa had apparently been friendly with some Roman Catholic priests in Salisbury, for one of his followers mentioned that he had received his Bible from a Catholic priest there (see File 2) although he himself had claimed to have obtained it from a shop in Salisbury (A5). In his personal statement to the CNC, Shoniwa had expressed a peculiar attraction to the Catholic Church in the following words:

> I associate myself with the Roman Catholic Church, although I have no permission of any representative of this Church to preach to natives on their behalf. It was my intention to gather natives around me and then ob-

tain the necessary authority of the Roman Catholic Church to have a separate native Church (A9).

Apart from his contact with the established Anglican, Methodist and Roman Catholic Churches, Shoniwa had also been subject to the impact of Christian teaching through a variety of other religious bodies, and the presence of such division in white Christianity must have left a strong impression on his mind. One of his followers suggested that he had wanted to be attached to the Catholic Church because he was given to believe that it was the largest of the Christian Churches!

Shoniwa seems to have been a person of very strong religious disposition, and one account mentions that he used to have religious dreams when he was young, and that he used to make crucifixes which he would then place within church buildings (B9). One of his followers related to me how Shoniwa used to like to dress up in the manner of a priest and stand before a self-made altar. In traditional Shona religious custom, the wearing of beads around the neck was very popular, and they were worn especially by the mediums of the different alien spirits (*mashave*) and by diviner-herbalists (*nganga*) (Gelfand, 1962, 149). Many Shona would also wear them as a protection against the threat of evil spiritual forces (Daneel 1971, 153). Shoniwa mentioned that he had been wearing three sets of rosary beads at the time of his religious experience (A6) and he would appear to have transferred a traditional belief to a biblical context. During his illness, he had lighted seven candles (A4) to dramatise the religious nature of his conversion experience and, when he had begun to proclaim his gospel in public, he was found wearing a white robe (on which a large red cross appeared), and he had in his possession a staff (at the end of which was attached a crucifix), and a Bible (A 5–6, B 51, 54, 64. See also Files 2, 4).

The date of Shoniwa's birth cannot be ascertained precisely, but he would seem to have been in his early twenties when his religious conversion took place in 1932. His followers claim that he was eighteen years old at the time, but this claim merely validates the highly dubious assertion that he was born on 1 October, 1914, the date on which Jehovah's Witnesses believed that the saviour would descend from the heavens. The CNC of Salisbury estimated in November 1932 that Shoniwa was about twenty-five years old then (File 5). Like so many other young Shona at the time, Shoniwa had moved to Salisbury in search of work towards the end of the 1920s and he described his varied experience as follows in 1932:

About four years ago, I paid my first visit to Salisbury and was issued with my first registration certificate. I obtained employment with Messrs H. Garmany & Co. as a leader to a waggon, remaining in this employment for eight months. I afterwards was employed as a kitchen boy by a Mr Wright, who lived in Second Street, for three months. I was next employed by an Indian in Bank Street for four months. For five months, I was employed by a Dutchman at Hatfield as a leader, and then [I] was employed by Mr Cambitzi at Arbennie as a garden boy for another five months. I then obtained employment for three months with a native named Gilbert, a carpenter of Salisbury (A2).

Shoniwa must have accumulated a wide range of experience during these years working for such a great variety of employers, and it was without doubt during this time that he had acquired so many manual skills which were to become so characteristic of his followers in later years. Carpentry was to continue to hold a very special place. Sailous Kutsanzira (see fig. 2, p. 35 and fig. 11, p. 115 below), the close friend of Shoniwa and the head-preacher of the Apostles at Gandanzara, told me that Shoniwa had set up a carpentry shop there in which he used to continue to work in the years following his conversion experience.

The hill on which Shoniwa had gone to pray after his religious experience is identified by his followers as Marimba. Marimba, in fact, refers to a range of hills near lake McIlwaine, and the hut in which Shoniwa had been living was at the foot of one of these hills.[6] Like John the Baptist, Shoniwa had gone into the wilderness (masowe) to pray, and so, his followers had begun to refer to him as 'Johane Masowe' (John of the wilderness), or simply as 'Baba Johane' (Father John). When he had come down from the hill, Johane had met a fellow African by the name of Andrea who lived at Nyamweda. He had asked Andrea to take him to Nyamweda and he had begun to preach to the people there with the permission of the chief (File 2). When he had succeeded in collecting a following, he had moved to the Hunyani river about ten miles away where he had continued to preach daily on the hill of Nyamatara near Elladale Farm (Files 2 and 4; see also map 2, p. 10). Andrea described the situation as follows:

> At this spot, we camped, males and females. Every day, John the Baptist preached in the same strain but did not baptise. At this place, I was instructed by John the Baptist to take confession. Several natives confessed that they had stolen mealies from the lands, [some confessed] that they had been immoral with women, some that they were witchdoctors, and several native unmarried girls said that they had had sexual intercourse with their sweethearts. After they had confessed, they were told that they would be baptised and forgiven for their sins (File 2).

---

[6] The location of the hill of Marimba which the Apostles refer to is about four kilometers east along Skyline Road which branches off from the main Salisbury–Bulawayo highway about forty kilometers from Salisbury. There is a government boundary marker on top of the hill today.

It was clear that Johane Masowe had been insisting on the necessity of repentance before baptism. He had begun to prepare the way of Jehovah, for the kingdom of heaven was near at hand (Mt. 3:2–3).

It must be remembered, however, that Johane's preaching was taking place in the aftermath of the severe economic depression which had spread throughout Mashonaland at the end of the 1920s (see pp. 6–8 above) resulting in an atmosphere of frustration and discontent in the midst of large-scale unemployment. His message of salvation was listened to by people who tended to see the whole of life and its various misfortunes through religious spectacles. As far as they were concerned, the white man's world—from which they had been excluded—was evil and would be overthrown. The coming of the kingdom of heaven meant that God was going to intervene to restore the goods which had been taken from the black man by the white man. In order to hasten this day, all black men would be required to separate themselves from the world of the white man and everything connected with it. The white Christian churches, which had failed to bring saving power to the black man, were to be shunned as well, and a return to the ways of their forefathers encouraged. These nativistic and millenarian tendencies were expressed in the report given by Andrea in the following manner:

> He [Johane] preached that he was John the Baptist sent by God to earth. He urged everyone present to adopt the religion of their forefathers, to drink plenty of kaffir beer and eat the meat blessed by our forefathers; further, that we should burn the religious books of the European, as our forefathers did not have books. He suggested that the Bible, hymn books and the New Testament should be destroyed, together with all other religious books. He promised that he would carry out baptising after which he [would] foretell the end of the world (File 2).

In a situation in which money was so scarce, a situation in which Africans were still expected to pay Government taxes (File 4) and church dues, Johane's message embodied an element of economic protest in particular. In an interview held with Johane, an African detective made the following report:

> I then asked him [Johane] if the European teaching with regard to religion was correct, and he replied that it was not good because they collect money; that is why he did not like the Bible or Testament because they were bought with money. This native continued and said that if all natives gathered at this spot, all the Europeans would go away in one night. . . . (File 4).

One of the reasons why Johane's directive not to use Bibles was, apparently, so well received at first seems to have been that it had removed the need for money in this respect. He was also very careful not to hold any form of church collection during his preaching sessions (File 2). In regard to Government authorities, he was equally careful not to say anything which might have seemed to be subversive (File 3) but he did insist on a policy of rejecting all the modern innovations introduced by the white people, whether they concerned education, medicine, agriculture or religion. By the end of 1934, he was still instructing people 'not to plough their lands, not to carry registration certificates, and not to work for the White people' (File 31). The means of obtaining victory were to come from heaven, and he had been telling people that God would supply them with food, that he himself 'wishes all natives to follow him, and [that] later, Moses and Elijah, the prophets, would come down from heaven and make war with the Europeans and drive them out of the country' (File 31). It is significant that the older people in general had been paying very little attention to Johane at that time. It was the young folk, those who had little stake in cultivation, who had been listening to him (File 32).

THE BIRTH OF AN INDIGENOUS AFRICAN RELIGIOUS MOVEMENT

After due investigation, the CNC in Salisbury had decided that there was nothing of a seditious or objectionable nature in the preaching of Johane Masowe. In fact, he had found him to be very co-operative in his manner, and 'his demeanour was quiet and respectful' (File 5). At the same time, he recommended that a close watch be kept on his activities in case any subversive features might develop. Johane was ordered to return to his own home district at Rusape and to remain there. This was at the beginning of November 1932.

It quickly became apparent, however, that Johane had had no intention of remaining outside of the Hartley district where most of his following was resident at the time, and he was arrested twice during the month of November for being in that district. The first time the charge was for failing to carry a pass (File 6), and the second time for failure to pay taxes (File 6). It would appear that he actually served the latter three-month sentence at Gatooma prison, for it has been recorded that he was released from there in March 1933 and escorted back to Rusape (File 8). A martyr syndrome had begun to develop around the person of Johane during this period of imprisonment—as had occurred in the case of the prophet Simon Kimbangu in the Congo after 1921—and his name was spread widely by his followers. His followers have preserved accounts of the wonders which he performed while in prison, particularly an incident in which pick axes began to work on their own while Johane rested. See also B 64–71.

Johane's fame had already preceded him to his own home district and, when he was released from prison, he had found many who were enthusiastic to listen to his teaching. During the following year, he had concentrated his preaching in the Makoni, Wedza and Marandellas districts (see map 2 on p. 10 above) where he had begun to consolidate his movement around his own extended family. The authorities had evidently continued to keep a close watch over his activities, for he was arrested five times within this period, viz., twice at Marandellas, twice at Rusape, and once at Buhera (Files 6, 8, 12, 13, 18, 28). The hill of Chinyamatamba in the Wedza district (where the Ruzawi and Chizawana rivers meet) had become a very important meeting place for Johane and his followers (File 10) and it was there that the first pentecost had occurred in which the holy spirit was believed to have descended on believers.[7] It was there also that Johane had first begun to baptise his followers. The Assistant Native Commissioner (ANC) of Wedza gave the following description of Johane's activities on the hill of Chinyamatamba in June 1933:

> Shoniwa gave out that he was John the Baptist, that he had been dead for three days and had been resurrected. He had received a divine message, he said, to call upon the native people to forego their evil ways, to give up witchcraft and the instruments and medicines appertaining thereto. He . . . called upon those present to hand in their *'miti'* [i.e., medicines] and instruments of witchcraft. This was done and a very large quantity of horns of medicine, small calabashes, witchdoctors' bones and other articles were handed in. The women and girls were called upon to hand in their adornments, bead necklaces, rings, gay kerchiefs and the like. The reason given for the handing in of these adornments was that evil would come from such vanities. Two sacks full of medicines, etc., were handed over (File 10).[8]

[7] Cyprian Nedewedzo described the incident to me as follows: 'One morning at about six o'clock while Baba Johane was on the hill of Chinyamatamba, he told the people that they should live in peace and that God would send them the holy spirit. It happened that about nine o'clock when the people were praying that they were all filled with the holy spirit and they were heard to speak in new tongues. All the alien spirits (*mashave*) came out of them and they spoke in this way: "We are running away; we are going; we are returning to the place from where we have come because the light has come with Baba Johane, the king of kings".'

[8] Daneel has pointed out that Evans Pritchard's distinction between witchcraft and sorcery among the Azande does not apply to the Shona. Hence he uses the term 'wizardry' to cover both witchcraft and sorcery. The Shona word *varoyi* may refer to either witches or sorcerers and the word *uroyi* may refer to the activity of both. Daneel writes: 'Unlike the Azande, both Shona witches and sorcerers are in possession of, and make frequent use of magical preparations (*mushonga*). The psychic act which distinguishes witches from sorcerers does not necessarily exclude the use of magical preparates' (1971:157). In the present work, I shall be using the term 'witchcraft' in the more general sense of Daneel's 'wizardry' to include the activity of both witches and sorcerers.

It is clear that Johane's teaching was expressed within a religious framework, and that he saw the main obstacle to salvation for Africans in the evils embedded in traditional forms of witchcraft. One of the crimes which he had reacted against most strongly, and which he had attributed to the power of witches, was the killing of unborn or newly born babies (B43-44). As a result of this, he had feared that they would not be able to enter heaven because they would never have had the chance of being baptised (B42). Johane had been very careful not to preach anything that might be considered either illegal or immoral by the authorities, a procedure which the ANC of Wedza believed 'tends to further convince the natives that he is divinely inspired' (File 10). His charismatic personality (see pp. 99-102 below) had continued to evoke a widespread response from those who came into contact with him, particularly among the young (File 10). They were easily impressed by his 'pseudo-miraculous prophecies' and the ANC even observed that 'when he arrived at this Office, the headmen who were here all saluted him' (File 10). Johane had 'warned that should they fail to carry out his words, God would be angry and would send no rain' (File 10). Such threats, based on the self-assurance of powers as great as those of any traditional religious functionary, commanded the obedience and respect due to charismatic authority. While the ANC still believed that Johane did not pose any form of direct threat to the authorities, yet this increasing demonstration of unquestioning obedience to Johane on the part of Africans had left him with a growing sense of uneasiness should this movement suddenly be diverted from its present course and become an instrument of rebellion. The factor which had really frightened the ANC, however, was not so much the presence of Johane's movement in itself, but rather the fact that the authorities had had no legal means at their disposal for preventing the growth of such movements. The ANC of Buhera had become particularly anxious about the situation when, in November of 1933, Johane and some of his followers—whom he described as 'a body of people consumed by religious zeal, out to defy constituted authority' (File 14)—had begun to preach in his territory. He had gone on to express his anxiety over the fact that 'with the exception of a form of "persecution" in having such sects—or their emissaries—brought up before the Native Commissioner for interrogation or issue of a vague warning, I am aware of no machinery authorising the taking of direct immediate action where thought desirable.'

APOSTOLIC FAITH MISSION AND WATCH TOWER

It has already been mentioned that two of the religious movements which had been a cause of concern to the Southern Rhodesian Government at the time were the Apostolic Faith Mission of South Africa which had established itself in Mashonaland, and Watch Tower (see pp. 9–11 above). It will now be seen how Johane and his followers had become the object of severe repression as a result of their presumed association with both of these bodies.

In the early 1930s the overseer of the AFM in Salisbury was a Mr L. L. Kruger and, as long as the church was controlled by a European leader, its authorised preachers had the right to move about in the Reserves. The followers of Johane Masowe had begun to refer to themselves as Apostles, hence being easily confused with adherents of the AFM. Furthermore, there were strong indications that many of those who had joined the AFM had since changed their allegiance to Johane. The ANC of Wedza wrote as follows in June 1933:

> The coming of Shoniwa coupled with the very obvious affinity which the adherents of the Apostolic Faith in this sub-district have for this charlatan have convinced me that the adherents of the Apostolic Faith in the Wedza Reserve are doing harm among the natives. There is no doubt that they are persuading young men and women, boys and girls, to leave established Churches and join their sect. ... That the Apostolic Faith adherents have associated themselves with his (i.e., Shoniwa's) teaching, have virtually allied themselves with him and are daily gaining more and more adherents in this district, in many cases taking away members of other Churches, are questions which, it is thought, need consideration (File 10).

Complaints had begun to pour in to the authorities from African chiefs and elders in many places, as well as from many of the established mission churches, in connection with the dangerous and immoral effect which certain preachers were having on the younger people (Files 7 and 10). It would seem that children were being drawn away from school in order to participate in the activities of these preachers, and young people were spending the nights on the hillsides in what were considered to be highly dubious circumstances (Files 11 and 15). Such preachers had begun to place major emphasis on the power of the spirit to take hold of people by entering into them, an emphasis which had found a natural basis in traditional Shona religious beliefs. Unsupervised preaching of this nature had tended to result in frenzied and immodest forms of activity (for example cf. Files 7, 9, 15, 16, 21, 23, 30). It will suffice to quote one example concerning one Tom Gutsa who had been a member of the AFM:

> Until some five or six months ago, his [i.e., Gutsa's] preachings appeared to have but little ill effect; since then, however, Gutsa appears to have encouraged a Shabi dance type of worship during which his congregation

are worked up into a religious frenzy shivering as though in fits, shouting and raving and becoming possessed by spirits and speaking in unknown jargons which the teacher gives out as other languages, even addressing pigs and other domestic animals in a language which it is stated by the teacher is thoroughly understood by the animal addressed. In other words, these people are induced to the belief that the spirit of God has entered into them in actuality, and that they are thus enabled to speak in many tongues. Inside and outside this church, the people, boys and girls, throw themselves on the ground in ecstacies of fervour and in many cases denude themselves of their clothing and rush about naked (File 20).

It would appear that aberrations of this kind had become rather frequent occurrences.

Notwithstanding the nature of the above complaints, however, the CNC tended to take a much more sympathetic view in regard to those who had found some sense of satisfaction in following Johane. He regarded his activities as 'merely the harmless ravings of a religious maniac' (File 11), and as long as Johane contained his activities within the religious sphere and did not break the law, the CNC insisted that 'there is religious freedom in this Colony, [and that] people can adopt any creed which appeals to them' (File 11). The CNC appears to have had a keen perception of the difficulties, frustrations and tensions under which rural Africans were labouring, and due to the confusion which the wide variety of white-controlled Christian denominations must have been causing, it did not seem strange to him that many should leave these bodies and join the Apostles of Johane Masowe. 'This merely indicates,' he wrote in July 1933, 'that their denominational creeds have not got a very strong hold on them. . . .' (File 11). In December of the same year, he expanded on this:

> That there should be a large number of Native Sects springing up all over the country, each one interpreting and warping Christianity to suit its own ends, does not appear to me to be surprising when we consider the example set by the Europeans who have brought this exotic religion to Africa. From the differences between the numerous Christian Churches in the Colony, not to mention the diverse attitude of European laymen towards the Churches, it must appear to Natives that we ourselves have no certain knowledge or conviction about the religion [which] the Churches are competing [for] and wrangling [about] among themselves to get the Natives to adopt (File 17).

In regard to a complaint from an Anglican Mission concerning the conduct of Johane's followers, the CNC wrote in March 1934 saying: 'I do not know how or why we should attempt to stop Natives singing and enjoying themselves in their own Reserves. If they cannot do this in the Reserves, where can they do it?' (File 19). In what concerned religion, then the CNC showed himself very liberal. On the other hand, he continued to insist that African religious movements be kept under constant surveillance lest they should take 'an objectionable political turn' (File 11). In April of the same year, the danger of such a turn had suddenly begun to loom large.

In the early days of his preaching, Johane had admitted to the authorities that he had known one Charles Mzengeli who belonged to the Independent Industrial and Commercial Workers' Union of South Africa (ICU). As a result of this contact, a fear had always remained in their minds concerning the extent to which the potentially subversive thought of this organisation might have influenced Johane, although he himself made little of the relationship (A8). Charles Mzengeli had become Organising Secretary of the ICU which had been established in Salisbury in 1929. Under the leadership of Clemens Kadalie, the ICU had challenged both the white establishment and the élite leadership of Congress in South Africa and, according to Ranger, it had become 'the most striking of all South African mass movements in the twentieth century' (1970, 149). It was basically a secular movement which regarded religion as a matter of private concern. It openly criticised the white ruler for failing to educate the African properly and for not paying him a satisfactory wage for labour rendered. Although it did not encourage the use of violence, the overall thrust of the movement was considered by the Rhodesian authorities to be highly dangerous. By 1930 it was being openly condemned by both the Native Administration and the established churches (Ranger, 1970, 149). In October 1932 Mzengeli had actually gone to the spot where Johane had been preaching at Nyamatara hill and, although he did not speak to Johane himself, he had openly encouraged the work which he had been doing. At this time, he had said to his followers:

> The Government is clever; they collect taxes from people. This is not sufficient for them [though]; they build churches and collect money that way also. Don't believe the white men of the Church. They turn their collars around the wrong way which means that they have forgotten about God. The piece of black limbo that they wear in front indicates that their hearts are black (File 4).

Whatever the effect of Mzengeli's outlook on Johane may have been, we do know that Johane did, in fact, protest against taxation for the upkeep of church buildings and blamed the white churches for their failure to carry out the work of God among Africans (B60–61).

On 21 April, 1934 the Assistant Chief Native Commissioner organised a meeting of African chiefs and headmen in response to complaints concerning 'objectionable pseudo-religious practices'. The result of the meeting was that the chiefs and headmen requested that the Government take action against these religious movements which, they believed, were doing such harm (File 21). Two days later, the ACNC wrote to the CNC to say that, in addition to the information received at the meeting, he had since learned that 'the state of considerable numbers of the Natives is such as may militate against the stability of the State—ultimately, if not immediately' (File 22). He went on to say that he had received certain information which had led him to believe that 'what began with religious hysteria is now taking a political bias which is anti-European'. A few days later, the CNC wrote to the Honourable the Minister of Native Affairs making specific reference to AFM, John the Baptist, and Watch Tower and suggesting that the Native Department 'be authorised to deal with them through the wide powers conferred by the Native Affairs Act' (File 24). The letter also included a recommendation concerning the prohibition of objectionable literature—a measure which would seem to have been directed against Watch Tower publications in particular.

On 10 May, 1934 more restrictive measures were taken against 'pseudo-religious sects and factions' by virtue of Circular Minute number twenty-three (File 25). Shortly afterwards, Mr Kruger and his colleagues in AFM were forbidden to enter the Native Reserves (File 27)—areas which, by virtue of the Land Apportionment Act of 1931, had covered more than twenty-eight million acres of land (Daneel, 1971, 55). Due to excessively harsh measures, however, taken by certain Native Commissioners, it became necessary to point out in August 1934 that steps should only be taken against 'pseudo-religious sects indulging in activities antagonistic to the welfare of the Natives and militating against the stability of the State' (File 29). It was further pointed out that there were many adherents of AFM who were entitled to reside in the Reserves. Consequently, Shona adherents of AFM—as well as the followers of Johane Masowe—had retained a large measure of freedom to preach in their own areas. At the same time, Johane Masowe himself had apparently found it increasingly difficult to move about without hindrance in Mashonaland. For the next few years, he had moved about secretly and had remained in hiding for long periods. Towards the end of the 1930s he made his way south to Matabeleland with the intention of even moving on to Zululand, if necessary, in order to be left free to preach the message which, he believed, had been entrusted to him by God for African peoples.

PRELIMINARY CONCLUSIONS

A large part of the material which has been considered in the foregoing pages has been taken from Southern Rhodesian police files, a factor which must be kept in mind when evaluating the activities of Johane Masowe and his followers. The authorities were not interested in the religious motivation which may possibly have been at work in Shona prophets and preachers, nor were they particularly concerned with the possible aspirations and needs which religious movements may have been fulfilling for their adherents. Such movements undoubtedly contained a great many elements which appeared to be harmful both to the State and to Africans themselves, but such judgments were made by white people who belonged to a very different cultural heritage than that of the people with whom they were dealing. The vantage point of the white observers, whether in the established mission churches or in seats of political government, was entirely different from that of an oppressed and confused African people. A white minority ruling power was in a rather questionable position to decide on what was for 'the welfare of the Natives', and it was only too ready to dub as 'pseudo-religious' or as 'sect' (with strongly negative connotations) any religious movement which appeared to be 'militating against the stability of the State'. The white established churches also were often only too ready, for their part, to dub as false or heretical any religious movement which might succeed in drawing away from their folds their hard-earned African Christians. Good will and upright intentions were not in question, but rather a certain failure at times to appreciate the need for Christianity to meet African peoples in a full human sense on a level which was relevant and meaningful as a saving power vis-à-vis their traditional religious heritage and current socio-religious problems and needs.

Johane Masowe's early followers appear to have been drawn mainly from the younger generation, but it would be rash to assume (on the basis of police files) that they were the only ones who had been attracted by his preaching. The message which he had proclaimed rested on a firm traditional religious basis, and a form of biblical revelation was being presented in an African way by an African prophet for African people within African thought patterns (see chapter III, pp. 46–50, below). Johane had presented his teaching in a religious framework which challenged many of the practices of the established white churches. A Methodist missionary in Southern Rhodesia in 1933 had given the following explanation for the number of members who had departed from his church to join the Apostles of John Maranke:

> The facing of a difficult task of keeping up collections has been too much for the faith of some of our members who have left our church to follow the leadings of some who claim to have a free, no-collection church with

no probationary period before baptism. This sect, led by some of those who in time past had to be removed from our own ranks because of sin, has caused great havoc at four or five of our stations.[9]

The followers of Johane Masowe would also appear to have been attracted by the absence of church dues, the opportunity for lapsed members of the established churches to become accepted, and the appeal of immediate baptism and admission without a period of probation. Behind all these reasons, however, would seem to have been the desire on the part of a great many Shona to be given a share in the power of the Christian spirit which the white churches had apparently kept to themselves. Looking back on the situation years later, a Masowe Apostle expressed this yearning in the following manner:

> When we were in these synagogues [i.e., the established white churches], we used to read about the works of Jesus Christ, how he sent out his disciples who visited all lands spreading the gospel and also placing hands on those who were sick. Cripples were made to walk and the dead were brought to life. Those with evil spirits were prayed for, and the evil spirits were driven out. People received the holy spirit. That is what was being done in Jerusalem. We Africans, however, who were being instructed by white people, never did anything like that. We just worshipped an idol. We were taught to read the Bible, but we ourselves never did what the people in the Bible used to do. We never did the works which were mentioned by Jesus Christ. Jesus Christ, however, gave power to his disciples.[10]

The early years of the Apostles of Johane Masowe bear many resemblances to religious movements which have been studied in other parts of the world, particularly those referred to as 'cargo cults' (Worsley, 1957; Lawrence, 1964; Cochrane 1970; Burridge, 1960; Mead, 1956). It has been pointed out that the material cargo is understood as a symbol for the transformation of an oppressed people into new men by bringing them status, prestige and moral integrity. Such movements usually contain strong millenarian features, features of the kind of movement which Burridge has described as one which 'envisages a dramatic and rapid transformation of a frustrating and deprived state into a rewarding and glorious state by religious means' (Burridge, 1969, 317, n.10. See also Thrupp (ed.) 1962). It has also been pointed out that such movements generally contain a strong emphasis on the return of the ancestors who will usher in the new era, and the prophet-founder or leader of the movement may take on messianic characteristics (Talmon, 1966, 159–200). Wallace has

---

[9] *Journal of the Rhodesia Annual Conference,* 1933, p. 103, quoted in Norman E. Thomas (1968), pp. 60–63.

[10] Extract from sermon delivered at St. Mary's Township, Salisbury, in 1974.

summed up the various types of nativistic, millenarian and messianic movements under the heading of 'revitalisation movements' (1956, 264–81).

The Apostles of Johane Masowe were a revitalisation movement in the sense that the movement did contain nativistic, millenarian and messianic features. It is very important, however, to observe carefully the manner in which these features were understood within a biblical framework. Johane did, at first, advocate a return to the ways of his forefathers, but, as Yinger has observed, 'Invention is often in the form of revelation to a prophet who proclaims the road not as something new, but as a return to the ways of the ancestors' (1971, 316–17). By insisting on such a return, Johane was emphasising his break with the white churches and their religion as embodied in the Bible. On the other hand, by emphasising his encounter with Jehovah, the God of the Bible—who was none other than the traditional Shona God who used to speak in the trees—he was presenting the biblical message in an African form. He himself was the messiah whom Jehovah had chosen to be a saviour to African peoples. His purpose was not to encourage traditional behaviour—in fact, he delivered a crippling blow to diviner-herbalists and to all forms of witchcraft—but rather to proclaim the new Judaeo-Christian message in African guise (see chapter III, pp. 46–50). Johane emphasised the end of the world as a counterpart to the coming of the kingdom of heaven as preached by John the Baptist. In this way, the downfall of the world of the white man was seen to correspond to the victory to be achieved by the black man. Victory, however, would be brought about by virtue of the religious power which was at work in Johane Masowe, the same power which had been at work in Moses, Elijah and John the Baptist. Johane Masowe never advocated the use of military power to overthrow the white man and his movement was one of passive withdrawal in this sense. Just as the Shona-Ndebele Risings of 1896–97 might be compared to the Ghost-Dance among the American Indians in this respect, so the Apostles of Johane Masowe might be compared to the development of the Peyote Religion (Mooney, 1965; Aberle, 1959, 74–83; Aberle, 1966; LaBarre, 1938).[11] The manner in which the Apostles of Johane Masowe have continued to develop, however—as will be seen in later pages—demonstrates the extent to which a biblical awareness had become a vital part of the movement.

[11] See also Yinger's use of the terms 'aggressive sects' and 'avoidance sects' in Yinger, *Scientific Religion*, pp. 275–8.

CHAPTER II

THE KORSTEN BASKETMAKERS

THE APOSTLES IN PORT ELIZABETH

Johane Masowe moved south to Matabeleland at the end of the 1930s and there he found large numbers of Ndebele waiting to be baptised. Although the Ndebele had never been on good terms with the Shona, the dynamic evangelist, Lazarus Chipanga, had preached the message of the Shona prophet with great success. The Shona and Ndebele had joined together once before in 1896–97 in military uprisings against a common white foe; now, they had responded together to the appearance of an African saviour. If the Ndebele tended to reject Johane as a Shona, many readily accepted his message and what he stood for as a God-sent messenger to African peoples.

The Apostles established their headquarters at Bulawayo where they began to organise themselves on a more secure basis. Positions of authority were allocated to various members and economic enterprises were undertaken. It was not long, however, before harassment from Government authorities and African chiefs began to interfere once again with the activity of the Apostles with the result that they had to look for some suitable place in South Africa to which they might move their headquarters. Johane himself and a number of his followers had already travelled to the Transvaal a number of times at the beginning of the 1940s, and numerous converts had already been made there through the preaching of an Ndebele-Zulu evangelist named Ernest Maposa who had formerly been a member of an African Zionist religious movement. The Apostles settled for a few years in the Transvaal moving between the location of Eastwood in Pretoria and those of Everton and Orlando in Johannesburg. These were years of great hardship, and the Apostles found it very difficult to eke out a livelihood. They also suffered harassment from the authorities there. Between 1943 and 1947, Johane had travelled south as far as Cape Town and east as far as Durban in an attempt to find a place where he and his followers might settle without disturbance. It was not until the end of the 1940s, however, that he finally settled with a small group of followers in the Korsten district of Port Elizabeth.

From 1947 onwards, groups of Masowe Apostles continued to join their founder in Korsten where his headquarters had then become established. Due, however, to the introduction of the Native Urban Areas Act 25/1945, Africans from Southern Rhodesia were prohibited under section twelve from entering an urban area in South Africa. As a provision, however, had been made excepting Africans domiciled in the Bechuanaland Protectorate (now Botswana), the Masowe Apostles approached the Bechuanaland authorities in the hope of obtaining the required documents. When this failed, they approached chief Moroka in Bechuanaland who was living close to the Southern Rhodesian border. This is the area, in fact, in which the Kalanga-Shona had been living (see map 1, p. 7 above). With his help, they managed to obtain Bechuanaland tax receipts with which they were permitted to remain in Korsten by the City Council of the Municipality of Port Elizabeth.

Johane Masowe had never placed much emphasis on the importance of money in itself as he had considered the end of the world to be very near. On the other hand, he had become painfully aware over the years of the manner in which his mission of preaching the gospel had suffered due to lack of economic security. He had seen how his apostolic work and mission had been seriously hampered by the fact that so much time had to be spent by himself and his evangelists and prophets (see pp. 102–8 below) in supporting themselves financially. Furthermore, it was important that his followers should be self-dependent in their work and self-sufficient in regard to the fulfilment of their material needs. Only thus, he believed, could they protect themselves from the corroding influences of the outside world on their new way of life and mission. The Masowe Apostles, therefore, set about the work of developing a wide variety of manual skills which they had brought with them from Southern Rhodesia. By 1955, they were already operating a small furniture factory of their own in Korsten and they were transporting furniture for sale to districts far away from Port Elizabeth as well as in the city itself; they had also become very enterprising in the production of tinware and baskets. Although basket-making was by no means their most important or most profitable form of industry, it was the one which had rendered them most conspicuous in the public eye. The Masowe women and children, as well as the men, played a large part in the production of baskets made from bamboo canes, and the white-clad female Apostles could be seen sitting around the Korsten village weaving their baskets or moving out on the streets of Port Elizabeth hawking them at very reasonable prices. It is for this reason that the Masowe Apostles became popularly known in Port Elizabeth as the 'Korsten Basketmakers', a name which has stuck to them ever since.[12] Although the majority of the Apostles are no longer

---

[12] For material dealing with the Basketmakers in South Africa, see the file on 'Basketmakers' at City Hall, Port Elizabeth; see also *Evening Post* (Port Elizabeth), 26 January, 1953; 27 February, 1953; 2 December, 1957; 24 January, 1958; 10 February, 1958; 12 June, 1958; 5, 7, 9, 13, 14 June,

engaged in basket-making today, they do not resent this title due to the pleasant memories which it holds for them of their former years in Korsten.

As the Masowe Apostles became more aware of themselves as an organised religious body, they gave themselves the formal title of the 'Apostolic Sabbath Church of God' and registered their factory as the 'Apostolic Sabbath Church Furniture Factory (Pty.) Ltd.' Later on, however, due to circumstances which are not quite clear, the factory went into liquidation as a result of which it was considered wise to change the name of the church to that of 'Africa Gospel Church'. The main area of Korsten occupied by the Basketmakers was to the west of what was known as the 'salt pan' or 'dry lake' (see map 3). It was bordered on four sides by Wells Crescent, Perl Road, Alex Street, and by Lange Street where the factory had been located. It was also in 15a Lange Street that Johane Masowe himself used to live.

In an article dealing with the African Independent Churches, Bengt Sundkler referred to Johane Masowe as the 'secret Messiah', and he related the following incident in which he had attempted to contact him in Korsten:

> I may have met him, but I do not know. We visited his group, a Shona Zionist colony, near Port Elizabeth. When I asked leave to meet the prophet or the bishop, I was told that he was away. But the very man whom I addressed may have been the Messiah, John Masowe or 'John of the Wilderness'. . . . He built a tightly-knit community which lives in an atmosphere of apocalyptic expectation around the Bantu Messiah. Known to his people, he remains unknown to the world at large. Officially, the community is ruled by a 'bishop', but this person is only a front, a *persona*, a mask, to the wicked world outside. Officially, the mask belongs to one J.S.; but this, too, is a mask because J.S. is really T.M. Behind the decoy of these masks, hidden in the white-robed mass of thousands of believers, is the real Messiah, John of the Wilderness (1961, 209–10).

This mysterious secrecy which surrounded Johane is one of the peculiar characteristics which remained with him up to the day of his death. It could be said that it was merely a hangover from his days of persecution in Southern Rhodesia, and that it had also become important not to reveal himself as a Shona immigrant in South Africa. On the other hand, he had continued to refrain from revealing himself

1962; *Eastern Province Herald* (Port Elizabeth), 16 February, 1953; 10 August, 1955; 7 July, 1958; 18, 19, 20, 24 September, 1958; 6 October, 1958; 20 February, 1959; 12, 16 May, 1959; 10 August, 1959; 5 September, 1959; 10 January, 1960; 14, 31 March, 1960; 20 April, 1960; 13 June, 1960; 4 November, 1960; 7 February, 1961; 6, 7, 8, 9, 11, 12, 14, 18, 26 June, 1962; *Daily News* (Durban), 1, 3 October, 1956; *Natal Mercury*. 7, 12 June, 1962; *Rand Daily Mail* (Johannesburg), 6, 7, 11, 12, 18 June, 1962; 26 September, 1962; *Sunday Tribune* (Durban), 6 February, 1955; 7, 14 October, 1956; 11, 25 November, 1956; 10 November, 1957, 7 August, 1960.

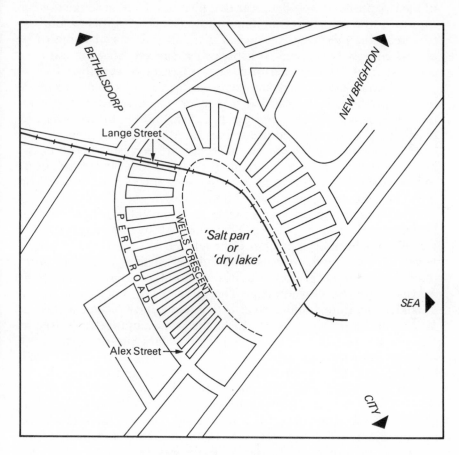

MAP 3. Korsten, Port Elizabeth, South Africa.

even in Zambia where the Apostles were later to be allowed to settle. His followers have told me that Johane would only reveal himself periodically to his followers and then to new converts only at the time of their baptism. It would appear that he himself had gradually ceased to preach to non-believers and had allowed his evangelists to continue to spread his message. His special work in public had come to be almost entirely concerned with baptising. Indeed, only he had been commissioned by God to perform this task (see pp. 91–3 below).

Whatever reason, then, may have motivated Johane not to reveal himself publicly, it is clear that he was not a person who sought for outward display of power and prestige. Even among his followers, he lived a very simple life and dressed as they did. The imminence of the end of the world was to continue to remain uppermost in his mind and he had very little interest in the things of this world. He appears never to have lost that sense of urgency to baptise as many Africans as possible before the day of judgment should arrive.

The Masowe Apostles have never used the title 'bishop' of their leaders but they were joined in Port Elizabeth by a Zulu called Elliot Gabellah[13] who used that title. Gabellah was known as the 'Spiritual Head' of the church to outsiders and he acted as a kind of communications manager for establishing good relations between the Apostles and the Government. The initials 'J.S.' and 'T.M.' which Sundkler mentioned above refer to the names Jack Sithole and Titus Muchuchu respectively. Titus Muchuchu was an evangelist of Johane Masowe and was, in fact, the same person as Jack Sithole. Jack Sithole was also known to outsiders as a leader of the church, and he and Gabellah worked together directing different aspects of the church's activity. When Gabellah left the Apostles in 1955, Jack Sithole was referred to as the main leader. This name, however, had a more subtle connotation for members, for Johane's father was named 'Jack', and the name 'Sithole' is the same clan name as 'Moyo' to which Johane belonged. In other words, Jack Sithole was really a synonym for Johane Masowe.

In 1951 a programme of slum clearance began in Korsten, a district which, after the Second World War, was undoubtedly one of the greatest slum areas to be found anywhere. While this programme was being carried out, a number of the Basketmakers were arrested for being in the urban area of Port Elizabeth without permits. This incident led to the inspection of the Basketmaker community in Korsten in January 1955 revealing the presence of six hundred persons. Of the

[13] Elliot Gabellah is, at the time of writing, Vice President of the African National Congress in Rhodesia, a medical practitioner in Bulawayo, and a priest of the African Orthodox Church.

172 male adults included, nineteen claimed to be Union-born, a hundred claimed to be from the Bechuanaland Protectorate and the remaining fifty-three claimed to be from Southern Rhodesia. It later became apparent, however, that those claiming to be from Bechuanaland were, in fact, of Southern Rhodesian origin. In June 1955 the Minister of Native Affairs ruled that the Basketmakers must leave the Union within six months in spite of a recommendation that they be allowed to move to another location in Port Elizabeth called Bethelsdorp where they had acquired some property. The decision was based on an amendment which had been made to the Native Urban Areas Act 25/1945 with the result that, by the mere addition of the word 'born', the 'MaShonas' (as they were also called) had become officially classified as illegal immigrants.

The date set for the departure of the Basketmakers from the Union was, in fact, postponed twice. In the meantime, it was reported that they had made an application to enter Israel:

> Because their religious beliefs and strict code of living are based on the Jewish faith, they say they are Jews. The head of the community, Mr Jack Sithole, first approached the Port Elizabeth offices of the Zionist Association. He learnt that such an application was out of the Zionist Association's province and was advised to apply to the Israel Embassy in Pretoria. It is understood here that the Israeli Minister will deal with the application and that it is being seriously considered (*Sunday Tribune*, 25.11.56).

However preposterous such a move may have seemed to outsiders, to the Basketmakers themselves it was very consistent with their religious conviction of being the new Israelites journeying towards Jerusalem. Although the application was finally rejected, it did not deter them from pursuing the goal determined on by their founder.

By December 1957 all of the slum dwellers had been moved from the Korsten district with the exception of the Basketmakers. Their departure had once again been delayed due to on-going discussions between the Governments of South Africa and of Southern Rhodesia concerning the question of repatriation. In 1959 the Southern Rhodesian Government sent an official delegation to South Africa in order to establish the fact that the Basketmakers were of Southern Rhodesian origin (*Eastern Province Herald*, 10.8.59). In August 1960 permission was finally granted for the Basketmakers to return to their country of origin along with their Union-born wives and children. A new turning point had been reached in their history as they prepared to leave the place which had left an indelible mark upon them. It was, in fact, almost two years later, however, before their deportation actually took place.

Port Elizabeth is more than just a name to the Masowe Apostles. To those who had lived there, it continues to stir up nostalgic memories; to those who had never been there, it is surrounded by a mysterious quality. When outsiders refer to them as the 'Basketmakers', they are proudly reminded of their days in Korsten. Notwithstanding the slum conditions of Korsten, the Masowe Apostles look upon these years as years of prosperity and peace, years in which they were not troubled by outsiders, years in which they had become organised on a secure and stable basis. It was there that they had come to regard themselves as an officially established church with officially recognised ministers. Membership cards were printed and distributed to all so that they might be able to obtain exemption from pass laws and travel concessions (Sundkler, 1961, 79). An official church stamp was also designed which comprised a seven-branched candlestick mounted on a globe with the map of Africa facing outwards (see fig. 2 on p. 35 below).[14] The Bible text referred to was Rev. 4:5 which says, '. . . and there are seven lamps of fire burning before the throne, and these mean the seven spirits of God.' The symbolic significance of the stamp is that the Apostles are the light of God to Africa.

DEPORTATION FROM SOUTH AFRICA

On 7 June, 1962 the first trainload of Basketmakers arrived at Plumtree in Southern Rhodesia. From there, they were moved to a temporary reception camp which had been erected at Mutunduluka about seven miles away. The last trainload arrived on 16 June and the total number of Basketmakers deported from South Africa had come to 1,880 persons.[15] The total cost of transportation was borne by the South African Government and no custom duty was charged on the Basketmakers' personal belongings when entering Southern Rhodesia

[14] In a private conversation with Elliot Gabellah, he told me that it was he himself who had designed the church stamp. When I asked him what it meant, he said: 'I was thinking about the word of God overlapping the globe and going right round the world, not being restricted to any particular area. The candlestick was symbolic of the holy place, the Holy of Holies. In the Hebrew set-up, the number seven is quite important and therefore there are seven lights to enlighten the world.'

[15] For material on repatriation of Basketmakers to Southern Rhodesia, see especially *Rhodesia Herald* (Salisbury), 6–8, 14–16, 21 June, 1962; 5 July, 1962; 9, 13, 18, 31 August, 1962; 27 February, 1963; 29 March, 1963; 10 April, 1963; 1, 11, 22–23 May, 1964; *Sunday Mail* (Salisbury), 10, 17 June, 1962; 23 June, 1963; 5 April, 1964; 24 May, 1964; *Daily News* (Salisbury), 6, 7, 11, 13, 20, 21, 23 June, 1962; 9, 20, 21, 24 August, 1962; 5, 16 November, 1962; 3 December, 1962; *Chronicle* (Bulawayo), 6, 8–9, 14–16, 21 June, 1962; 7 August, 1964; *Sunday News* (Bulawayo), 10, 17 June, 1962.

The Africa Gospel - Head Office: P.E.

Fear God and give glory to Him. Rev. 14 - 6 - 9

Preacher·Certificate

The Founder is John the Baptist 1932, on Mount Marimba.

This is to Certify that bearer hereof PREACHER ... *C.S. Kutaanjiva x659* ...

Address *Rusape Gandanzara ... Trubori* ... No. 211

has been anointed by the Holy Spirit, and is ordained as an approved Lord's Worker in the Africa Gospel.

To all Police in Africa. Please let him pass, he has been Approved by the word of Our Lord and his co-workers, to do the work of Our Lord in Africa and Overseas.

Under the protection of the Almighty God Our Lord, to go all over Africa and Overseas and the Lord be with you in His Work.

Go all over NORTH, SOUTH, EAST and WEST of Africa and Overseas, Day and Night.

IT GIVES HIM AUTHORITY

"To preach Gospel to the believers and unbelievers for Second Coming of Our Lord"—G.3.8, Matthew 24.14, 2 Pet. 1 - 18 - 21.

"To look after the Congregation"—Acts. 6 - 3.

"To Keep the Ten Commandments"—Malak 4 - 4. Deut. 5.6 - 2.

"To lay hands on, anoint and pray for the sick"—Mark 16 - 18. James 5 - 15.

"To bury the dead"—Rev. 14 - 13.

Minister *J.Cithole*

Secretary *Lupaciren Ngah*

Date *14.11* 1960

To all Railway Administrations, Harbours and Air Port Authorities in Africa.—Please give bearer a ticket as he has to do the Lord's Work in Africa and Overseas.

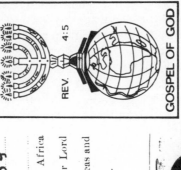

REV. 4:5

GOSPEL OF GOD

REV. 4:5

24-17

Fig. 2. Membership card and church stamp.

(*Rhodesia Herald*, 10.4.62). They regarded this, as they did many other incidents, as due to the power of Johane himself. They had, in fact, continued to pay taxes to the Bechuanaland Government during their years in Port Elizabeth and they were later assured by the Government Secretary of Bechuanaland that their tax money would be repaid if they could supply sufficient proof of their domicile there and of the amounts paid (*Sunday Mail*, 10.6.62).

The Basketmakers were offered a choice of three possible sites for resettlement in Southern Rhodesia, viz., Seki outside Salisbury, Zimunya outside Umtali, or Ntabazinduna outside Bulawayo (*Daily News*, 20.6.62). Mr H. J. Quinton, the Minister for Native Affairs, gave them until 16 August to make a decision after which time their free food supplies would be cut off. When they had failed to come to a decision by that date, Mr Quinton insisted that they move to Seki as 'it had been demarcated as an African Township for some years, and considerable development money has already been spent on the laying on of water supplies' (*Daily News*, 20.8.62). One hundred acres of land was being made available to them free of rent for three years. After this time, they would have the opportunity of either purchasing the land or leasing it from the Government. The Basketmakers continued to express their discontentment with this arrangement due to the fact that Seki was so far away from Salisbury where they might hawk their products as they had done in Port Elizabeth. Hence they refused to move for another few months until, finally, in the early months of 1963, a limited number of the total community began to settle in their new home at Seki Township.

The greater part of the Basketmaker community, however, had made it clear from the moment they arrived in Southern Rhodesia that they did not want to remain there. They had retained too many bad memories of the persecution suffered during the years before they had left and they had no desire to remain in a country which was still under white minority rule. Johane himself had made it clear to his followers that they would not be sufficiently free in such a situation to carry out their mission of preaching freely to Africans in other countries. In August 1962, they had expressed publicly their desire to move to an independent African State and had even threatened to send a delegation to the United Nations in order to obtain assistance for such a move (*Daily News*, 24.8.62). Mr Quinton, for his part, had assured them that he had no objection to granting them travel documents to go to other countries and he said that he would willingly allow the whole community to move to any country which was willing to accept them (*Daily News*, 20.8.62).

Towards the end of 1962 preparations were being made in

Northern Rhodesia for the elections which would install the first African Government there. The Basketmakers applied to the United National Independence Party representatives for permission to settle in Northern Rhodesia and the required permission was granted. By the beginning of 1963 large numbers of Basketmakers had spread out throughout the country particularly in the sub-urban areas of Lusaka and the towns of the Copperbelt. They established their headquarters at Marrapodi compound about two miles outside Lusaka.

When the Masowe Apostles first arrived in Northern Rhodesia, they were welcomed by large numbers of their own who had come there directly from Southern Rhodesia in 1947 and 1949. Many had settled in Mumbwa where there was very good farming while others had remained in Lusaka. One of those who had come in 1947 was Peter Chikono. Chikono had by 1963 established himself rather securely in Northern Rhodesia and, because of this, he was asked to act as a kind of public relations officer between the Apostles and the Government. It was he who formally registered their religious movement in Lusaka on 14 May, 1963[16] under the title 'Africa Gospel Church' just seventeen months before Northern Rhodesia became the Republic of Zambia on 24 October, 1964. Chikono took up his dwelling at Marrapodi where he became known to outsiders as the Head or Minister in Charge of the Apostles in a manner similar to that in which Elliot Gabellah had become known as the 'Spiritual Head' of the Basketmakers in Port Elizabeth (see p. 32).

The Masowe Apostles continued to flourish during the 1960s, consolidating their newly formed congregations throughout Zambia and founding new congregations elsewhere. They moved into Kenya in 1967, into Mozambique in 1969, and into Zaire in 1972. In the meantime, Johane Masowe had become very ill in Dar-es-Salaam, Tanzania, where he had settled in 1964, an illness from which he never recovered. It is not clear what the nature of the illness was but church records state that it caused a stiffening of the left side of the body. Johane would never allow himself to be hospitalised or to be given medicines as he believed that God would cure him at the appointed time. He remained adamant in this belief right up to the end. Johane died on 13 September, 1973 and the cause of death was officially stated as cardiac failure.[17] During his illness, which lasted nine years, Johane had spent one year at Dar-es-Salaam, seven years at Arusha, and the remaining year at Nairobi. All this time, he was attended by a small group of

---

[16] See Certificate of exemption from registration, Form S.O.3 RS/6660, Office of Registrar of Societies, Lusaka, Zambia.

[17] See Medical Certificate issued by the Ministry of Health, Ndola, 22 September, 1973.

Apostles which included a few elders, his three wives, a few Sisters (see pp. 62–9 below) and a few young male Apostles. It had always been understood that no one could come to see him unless sent for and, during these years, very few people were sent for. Johane had not wanted others to see him in such a weak and ailing condition.

During the last few years before Johane died, an atmosphere of discontent had been growing among the younger Apostles. This unrest came to a head with Johane's death in 1973 and resulted in the largest split which the Apostles have ever experienced. The breakaway group was led by Peter Chikono and the main source of grievance was centred on the control of power. The nature of the split will be considered more in detail on pp. 110–14 below. Both groups were accusing one another of being responsible for the death of Johane, and confusion on this issue had caused the split to spread throughout almost every congregation.

CONFLICT WITH THE ZAMBIAN GOVERNMENT

The Zambian Government had become particularly perplexed by the internal strife which had arisen among the Masowe Apostles during the last quarter of 1973 and which continued throughout the whole of 1974. As the Shona members had been officially authorised to settle in Zambia, and as freedom of religious worship had been constitutionally guaranteed to any lawful religious body, the Government had not wished to interfere in the internal politics of the church nor to take any active steps against its members. The occurrence of certain incidents of violence among members, however, had eventually left the Government with little choice other than to threaten the Apostles with the suspension of all their religious activities and with possible expulsion from Zambia.

During the early 1970s Government attention had been drawn to the fact that Marrapodi compound in Lusaka (see fig. 3) was being used by the Apostles as a shelter for unlawful activities. The Shona living there were being referred to as 'Zvinopindirana',[18] a Shona term which referred to people who removed engines from cars and replaced them in other cars. The elders among the Apostles had become very concerned over the fact that certain young ones had become involved in such forms of illegal activity but they had failed to control them by the use of religious sanctions. They had subsequently arranged with the Zambian Government to have some of themselves officially appointed

---

[18] See Philip Chirwa, 'Focus on "Zvinopindirana,"' *Zambia Daily Mail* (Lusaka), 8 March, 1974, p. 6.

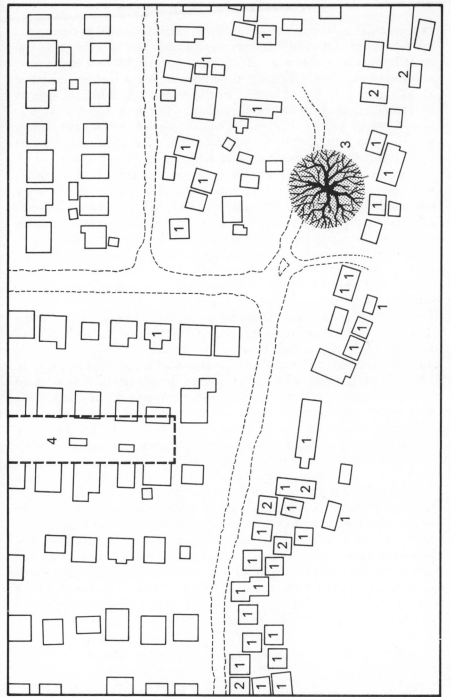

FIG. 3. A section of Marrapodi, Lusaka. *Key*: 1 Carpenter, 2 Tinsmith, 3 Fig tree, 4 Sisters' enclosure.

as constables to patrol their own district. This measure, however, had not succeeded either. In February 1972 a gathering of three thousand Apostles was held at Marrapodi at which the expulsion of four young members was publicly announced—a decision which had been reached at a Council held by the leaders of the Apostles in Botswana shortly beforehand and which had been ratified by Johane Masowe himself as he lay sick in Arusha, Tanzania. The outcome of this announcement was that the four members concerned had initiated a campaign of open revolt against the elders which had resulted in the split.

On 20 January, 1974 trouble broke out at Marrapodi in which shots were fired, people were injured, and houses and cars were damaged.[19] The elders claimed that they were being forcibly threatened and assaulted by some younger members. Similar outbreaks of trouble arose on the Copperbelt in Kitwe and Ndola towards the end of January.[20] Ndola had, in fact, become the headquarters of the young breakaway group which will henceforth be referred to as the 'rebel group' led by Peter Chikono as distinct from the 'loyalist group' led by evangelist Cyprian Nedewedzo Nhamburo Nyati (see fig. 10, p. 113 below). Both groups were claiming lawful succession to their founder and both insisted on retaining the formal title of 'Gospel of God' church, a title which had replaced that of 'Africa Gospel Church' in 1972. The Zambian Government was thoroughly confused by the split. It was Peter Chikono who had registered the church in 1963 whereas the elders were now claiming that he had usurped the position of the founder. A stalemate had been reached.

The loyalist group arranged to hold a Synod at Gandanzara in Rhodesia in September 1974 to clarify the question of succession. Gelfand has written that among the Shona, 'when a chief dies, his successor is not appointed until a full year has passed' (Gelfand, 1959, 203), and this was, undoubtedly, the reason for choosing this date. The decision reached was that a council of seventy elders—none of whom should be less than fifty years old—should be appointed as the supreme authoritative body from then on. The number was most probably based on Ex. 24:1. The rebel group, on the other hand, had presented the Zambian Government with a new constitution which emphasised the democratisation of their authoritative structure. By the end of 1974, the troubles between the two groups of Apostles were still at a high point in Zambia (*Times of Zambia*, 25.9.74).

[19] See *Zambia Daily Mail* (Lusaka), 22 January, 1974. See also ibid., 24 January, 1974; *Times of Zambia* (Ndola), 22, 24, 25 January, 1974.

[20] See *Times of Zambia*, 28 January, 1974; *Zambia Daily Mail*, 29 January, 1974.

THE BURIAL OF JOHANE MASOWE

Although Johane Masowe had died in Ndola, Zambia, on 13 September, 1973, it was two weeks later before arrangements had been made to have the remains flown by air to Rhodesia. The corpse was sent in a wooden coffin which had been supplied by the rebel group among whom he had died, and the police in Salisbury had been alerted to the fact that there might be an outbreak of trouble among the Apostles in Rhodesia when the coffin arrived. Consequently, when the remains finally arrived on the evening of 27 September, they were escorted directly to the funeral parlour by the police. According to the loyalist Apostles, Johane had stipulated that he should be buried in a coffin with a glass top—possibly in the belief that he would be able to see the Lord at the Second Coming in which he so firmly believed. With this in mind, the loyalist Apostles in Rhodesia had purchased such a coffin and on the morning of 28 September they had transferred the corpse into it. The funeral cortege then left Salisbury for Gandanzara, near Rusape, where Johane Masowe was buried.[21] Thousands of Apostles from both groups had gathered there for the burial, and fighting would certainly have broken out were it not for the presence of the police in sufficient strength. A bitter argument arose as to which coffin the remains should be buried in—a matter of considerable importance to the Apostles on account of the question of lawful succession which it implied. The police finally intervened, and it was decided to bury both coffins. Later, however, it was discovered that both coffins would not fit in the grave and the wooden coffin of the rebel group was broken up into pieces and thrown in with the other coffin. Johane was not buried underground but in an altar-like structure which had been erected on a large flat rock on the top of Dandadzi hill and which had been covered over with cement (see fig. 4). On top of his grave were inscribed the words:

Ngirosi ye Africa [Angel of Africa]
Wakafa 13.9.73 [Died 13.9.73]
Kuwigwa 28.9.73 [Buried 28.9.73][22]

On the top of a small hill opposite to that of Dandadzi can be seen a small wooden cross which (the Apostles claim) had been used by Johane for baptisms and had been placed there by him before he had left Mashonaland. Some Apostles have told me that this cross remains

[21] Map reference to grave of Johane Masowe: VQ 371–318, Rusape. Scale 1:50,000. For eyewitness account of burial, see report at police station, Rusape, Rhodesia.

[22] In a report on the Synod drawn up by an Apostle, the spelling was changed to the more grammatically correct *yakafa* for *wakafa*, and *yakawigwa* for *kuwigwa*.

FIG. 4. The grave of Johane Masowe, Gandanzara, Rhodesia, 1974.

at an angle whenever there is trouble among themselves. The Apostles
have always attributed such mysterious qualities to objects connected
with Johane's God-given mission.

The Synod of loyalist Apostles which was held at Gandanzara from
24 September to 2 October, 1974 was not only intended to decide on
the question of succession but also—in accordance with traditional
Shona religious custom—to complete the burial rites and decide on
the proper allocation of the wives and property of the deceased
(Daneel, 1971, 101–103). The countries represented were: Rhodesia,
South Africa, Botswana, Zambia, Malawi, Mozambique, and Kenya.
The total number present was 16,500 people, of whom two thousand
were elders (i.e., ordained members) including 135 heads of congregations. A breakdown of the latter revealed that seven were
evangelists, 121 were preachers, five were prophets, one was a
'teacher', and one was a councillor.[23] A select group of Sisters[24] was
also present.

On the death of Johane Masowe in 1973, an era had passed in the
history of the Apostles. They had become established in nine different
African countries (i.e., Rhodesia, South Africa, Botswana,

[23] For a discussion on the different roles, see chapter V below, pp. 102–108.
[24] See chapter III below, pp. 62–9, especially pp. 67–9.

Mozambique, Zambia, Tanzania, Malawi, Kenya, and Zaire).[25] Accurate figures are notoriously difficult to gather on religious movements in Africa and, in the case of the Masowe Apostles, one is dependent at present on figures estimated by members themselves. The General Secretary of the Masowe Apostles in Nairobi claimed in early 1975 that their total number exceeded half a million—not taking into account the split which had occurred. He claimed that accurate figures were kept for the first time when Johane had conducted his baptismal tour begun in 1959 and that the total number of those baptised in Southern Rhodesia alone, had come to ninety-five thousand (fifteen thousand of whom had been baptised in the Bulawayo district).[26] Large numbers had also been baptised at this time in Northern Rhodesia and Nyasaland. The total estimate of Masowe adults and children in Rhodesia was reckoned at 500,000 over ten years ago in 1962. Irrespective of the accuracy of such figures, however, the Masowe Apostles have

[25] List of Masowe congregations in 1974 (obtained from the secretary of the Apostles at the headquarters in Lusaka, Zambia, 1974).

Rhodesia: Gandanzara, Bulawayo, Sawe, Semubengo, Sinoia, Gwamayaya, Guwe, Masango, Magunje, Mrewa, Mawangwe, Chimbudzi, Mkambirwa, Mdango, Shabani, Karoi, Umtali, Hartley, Betera, Raffingola, Randasi, Munyoro, Gutu, Shashabukwa, Chatsuwetsi, Bamgo, Rusape, Harare, Mtoko, Chiweshe, Vumbunu, Bonde, Gwanda, Dikilisi, New Area Wankie, Gokwe, Lupani, Gatooma, Zwimba, Nherera, Nyangombe, Dewedzo, Chipwatsura, Concention, Victoria Falls, Gwai, Date Wankie, Nkai, Chikwira, Buhera, Fumigwe, Kafusi, Gholi, Norton, Seki, Mapanzure, Gwelo, Nyoro, Shawa, Jenjera, Headlands, Zimunya, Vimba, Jindwi, Njanja, Marandellas, Macheke, Gwatemba, Sipolilo, Beatrice.

Botswana: Francistown, Lobatse, Serowe, Shashi, Moroka, Dambrok, Pikwe Mine, Madinare, Palapye, Gaborones.

South Africa: Mafeking, Everton, Rustenburg, Port Elizabeth, East London, Transkei, Durban.

Zambia: Lusaka, Livingstone, Kafue, Mumbwa, Kabwe, Ndola, Kitwe, Kalulushi, Chililabombwe, Lundazi, Nyimba, Rufunsa, Chipata, Kasama, Mbala.

Malawi: Blantyre, Mzimba, Nkata Bay, Mzuzu.

Tanzania: Arusha, Dar-es-Salaam.

Kenya: Nairobi, Meru, Machakos, Nyahururu, Basin Gishu, Kakamega, Narok, Kajiado, Nyandarua, Kisumu.

Mozambique: Vilapery.

Zaire: Lubumbashi. See also map 4.

[26] Figures concerning the total number of Masowe Apostles.
(Obtained from the Secretary General of the Apostles in Nairobi, Kenya, in March 1975)

Country	Year	Adults only	Adults and children
Rhodesia	1962		500,000
Zambia	1972	7,000	
Botswana	1972	3,000	
South Africa	1972	2,000	
Tanzania	1972	1,000	
Zaire	1972	1,000	
Kenya	1972	3,000	
Malawi	1972		2,000
Mozambique	1972	?	?

[Concluded overleaf

evidently reached a size which renders their presence and activity significant for the future of religion in Africa.

Peter Chikono died in November 1975, an occurrence which greatly weakened the stance of the rebel group of Apostles. Since then, the tension between the two groups has, in fact, eased considerably. The loyalist Apostles held their Synod at Gandanzara in September–Ocotber 1975 as they had done in 1974 and preparations had been made for another in 1976. More recent developments among the Masowe Apostles include the formal registration of the Gospel of God Church in Rhodesia, the dispatching of a member to London with the intention of establishing a congregation there, and plans for building a convent and a trade centre at Gandanzara—the former for the training of Sisters in Rhodesia and the latter for the training of members in the various manual skills.

Notwithstanding the split among the Masowe Apostles today, what is manifestly clear is that they, like so many other indigenous African religious movements, express the strength and vitality of a creative response to the Judaeo-Christian Bible as they have understood it and have appropriated it in their own lives in a relevant and meaningful way as members of vital religious communities.

List of evangelists

RHODESIA: *Dewedzo*: Daniel Mutunhire, Cyprian Nedewedzo, Julias Kadungure, Jethro Kuchenga, Savaniya Mashiri, Lazarus Chipanga, Abraham Bvekerwa; *Gandanzara*: Joseph Kanyongo, Obed Muchuchu, Alexander Chambara, Zebediah Chikuruwo Munatsi, Stephen Chichoni; *Masango*: Luka Chipendo, Standrech Madomombe Esvero Musangaza, Jameson Maposa, Joseph Seremwi, Philip Ndoro, Josiah Gura, Patrick Deka, Paul Brokeri; *Chikwira*: Thomas Watura, Paul Kamudariwa, Jeremiah Nhira, Frederick Kandawasvika, Willie Magaya; *Mrewa*: Joseph Manyepo, Isaac Chikukwa, Thomas Rusiku; *Njanja*: Obed Kuchena; *Umtali*: Luka Mutanguro, John Kupangwa, Weston Vumbunu, Josiah Magwindiri; *Buhera*: Josamu Nyamukapa, Josiah Tekere; *Gutu*: Samson Dauramanzi, Jonkias Mutinima, Samuel Chikomwe; *Bulawayo*: Ernest Maposa, Willie Ncube, Bunhu Moyo, Mapiki Moyo, Mawewe Bvula, Koli Sibindi, Masuku, Chuma, Jeremiah; *Chipinga*: Saizi Sithole; *Mashayamombe*: Philip Gudo, James Gore, Samuel Manogara; *Harare*: Simende Mazarura. ZAMBIA: *Lundazi*: Moses Banda, John Banda. MALAWI: *Mzimba*: Jordan Chikorosa, Lazarus Tswantswani. SOUTH AFRICA: *Mafeking*: Khiyoni Kilinjani.

Note: Nineteen evangelists have died since the church began, and seven others have left the church, namely Daniel Mutunhire, Josiah Gura, Esvero Musangaza, Philip Ndoro, Paul Kamudariwa, Alexander Chambara and John Kupangwa. No new evangelists have been ordained since the death of Johane Masowe. It still remains to be seen whether the supreme council of seventy at one of their annual Synods at Gandanzara may decide to appropriate to themselves the power of ordaining evangelists. The lack of new evangelists is already beginning to cause a crisis in the organisational structure of the church.

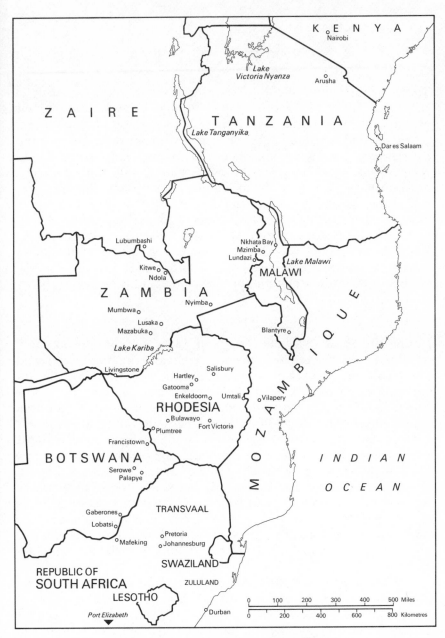

MAP 4. East, Central and South Africa.

CHAPTER THREE

CENTRAL BELIEFS

The religious beliefs of the Masowe Apostles are all centered upon Jehovah's choice of African peoples through their saviour, Johane Masowe. Their understanding of the role of their prophet-founder is based on traditional thought patterns but their conscious religious awareness is strongly biblical in both orientation and intent. Masowe religious belief, then, involves four separate, but interconnected, aspects which pivot upon the mediating role of Johane Masowe, viz., (1) Johane Masowe as the expression of the spirit and of the word of God, (2) the record of 'The Good News of Johane Masowe for Africa' as proof of the authenticity of Johane's God-given mission, (3) the Bible as the written word of God for African peoples brought by Johane, and (4) the collective body of Sisters as the visible sign and symbol of the presence of the spirit of God with his people.

1. THE ROLE-IDENTITY OF JOHANE MASOWE

During the Shona-Ndebele Risings of 1896 and 1897 in Southern Rhodesia, resistance had been particularly strong in central Mashonaland, and paramount chief Makoni had been one of the key figures (Ranger, 1967, 270). Central Mashonaland had been part of the Rozvi confederation and traditional spirit mediums—who had been closely connected with the Rozvi kings—had still continued to exercise a ritual superiority over the Shona paramount chiefs. Ranger (1967, 289) mentions that the Rozvi were probably important in the Maungwe area—an area to which Johane Masowe had claimed association—because the holder of the Rozvi title, Tandi, whose presence was required at the installation of a Makoni, was living there. As Johane Masowe was, in fact, a Tandi from the Makoni district, we can be sure that the influence of traditional Shona religious beliefs must have played a major part in conditioning his religious awareness and outlook.

All Shona peoples did not share a common religious belief system (Daneel, 1971, 29; Bourdillon, 1973, 11), although in the course of time, a process of syncretisation seems to have taken place between the two most widespread cults, viz., the cult of the High-God, *Mwari*, and the cult of the tribal ancestral spirits (*mhondoro*) who were approached through official spirit mediums (*vasvikiro*) (Daneel, 1970, 24–5). On the other hand, the syncretisation of the two cults 'never led to a complete identification of *Mwari* with Chaminuka' (Daneel, 1970, 25), the most prominent ancestral spirit who acted as 'the great messenger, the link between God and the people' (Gelfand, 1959, 13). Many Shona believed that Chaminuka had, in fact, emanated from the High-God himself and they had come to think of him as the 'son of *Mwari*' (Daneel, 1970, 24). The High-God was believed to be a transcendent God who remained distant from his people and retained complete control over his creation (Daneel, 1971, 80–83). Although he was normally believed to reveal himself in the powers of nature, such as in lightning, in the clouds, or in a shooting star from the heavens (Daneel, 1971, 82), he had also come to be regarded as a personal Being (Daneel, 1971, 83).

In the traditional Shona cult of the High-God, *Mwari* would communicate with his people through a female spirit medium (*mbonga-svikiro*) who was regarded as the voice of God. During oracular sessions, the relationship between the two was considered to be so close that 'for the duration of the ceremony, God and medium assume a single and indivisible identity' (Daneel, 1971, 90). In the cult of the tribal ancestral spirits (*mhondoro*), their relationship to God was considered to be so close that 'what the *mhondoro* says and does is as good as if it were done by God' (Gelfand, 1962, 172), but the *mhondoro* communicated with the people through official spirit mediums (*vasvikiro*). The Apostles have told me that in the early days of his preaching, Johane used to say, 'The spirit says such and such', but that gradually he ceased doing this and began to speak in a normal tone all of the time as the voice of God.

Johane had believed at first that God had not wished him to get married, a belief which may well have been based on his awareness of himself as the *mbonga-svikiro* who was also looked upon as the 'wife of *Mwari*' (Daneel, 1971, 90). Later on, he would seem to have transferred this notion of ritual purity to the Sisters (see pp. 62–9 below) who were to become completely dedicated to God as his 'wives'. At an even later date, this concept would appear to have found biblical justification in Rev. 21:2 where the New Jersusalem is described as 'a bride adorned for her husband'. One ought not to underestimate the ability of the Shona, like most African peoples, to indulge in such mystical flights of thought; their awareness of spiritual realities is very keen and runs side by side with that of an awareness of the material world.

Johane Masowe is referred to by his followers as *izwi raMwari* (the word or voice of God) and as *mudzimu waMwari* (the spirit of God), both traditional concepts within the Shona religious belief system. Gelfand has noted that the Rozvi, who were considered to be God's chosen people and his ministers, 'used to hear God's voice speaking from the mountains, or trees, or rivers, and God was able to produce food and other things for them from the rocks and trees' (1959, 201; 1962, 51). When commenting on John 1:14–15 during a Sabbath prayer-service, one of the Apostles linked Johane to this myth in the following manner:

> Baba Johane came. Baba Johane was there. Even today, he is there. Even today, he is there. Johane was there. He is the one who used to be talked about by our forefathers who used to say that they heard a voice speaking from a tree. God is for our forefathers. God is for our forefathers who used to wear loincloth. Like ourselves, they used to cut their hair and let their beards grow long. They are the ones who heard the voice from the tree. The voice used to say, 'Come here', but nobody knew that it was God who was speaking. People used to say it was the spirits of the earth who were speaking. Our forefathers used to say that they were given thick porridge. They used to say, 'we were given red porridge, we were given rice, we were given milk, we were given everything'. They never knew that it was God who was giving these things to them. They used to say that these were the wonders of the earth, and that they were caused by the spirits of the earth. But you understand now what it was. The voice (word) has taken flesh; the voice has appeared as a person. It has become a person who has lived among you. Gloria! Gloria! You gathered to hear him. You gathered to hear him.[27]

Johane Masowe himself had mentioned in his personal statement (A10) that the voice which had called him to his new role as John the Baptist used to come to him through a burning bush, and there can be little doubt about the fact that he had superimposed, or, rather, creatively blended, the biblical scene of the call of Moses as described in Exodus 3:4 with the traditional myth referred to above.

The concept of possession by an ancestral spirit (*mudzimu*) was very familiar to the Shona, and the sign that someone was being possessed was generally shown by a prolonged physical and/or mental illness (Gelfand, 1962, 21; Daneel, 1971, 100). Johane Masowe experienced such signs before his conversion experience (A3) and he had clearly interpreted them in terms of the desire of some spirit to take possession of him. He himself tells us that he had been very devoted to reading the Bible both before and during his illness (A5) and he had become convinced that it was the spirit of the biblical God which had wished to possess him. God had wanted him, he believed, to inherit the spirit of John the Baptist (A4). Once he had accepted his new role, his illness

---

[27] Taped extract from sermon delivered at Marrapodi, Lusaka, on 17 August 1974. Cf. Gelfand, *Religion*, pp. 154–55.

had disappeared (A11) in confirmation of the authenticity of his calling. Later on, Johane became convinced that God wanted him to inherit the spirit of Jesus as well. He was being called to perform the work of both John the Baptist and of Jesus for African peoples.

The traditional Shona concepts of the word of God and of the spirit of God came to be applied to Johane in a biblical context and, as an Apostle expressed it during a Sabbath prayer-service, 'the spirit of God descended from heaven, the word of God . . . [and] it came and rested on him'.[28] Another speaker expressed it like this that same day:

> God loved us, we in Africa, and he descended to Africa himself. He sent his messenger to Africa just as it had happened in the land of the Jews where Jesus Christ had been sent. Some people had been saying, 'God will come again as a white man', but God does not discriminate between black people and white people. Now, when we talk about God here, we mean the spirit of God (mudzimu waMwari). The spirit descends on whomsoever it wishes because everyone has been created by God.

The God in whom the Apostles believe is still the God of their forefathers but he has now revealed himself as Jehovah. Formerly, he had made himself known to the Hebrew people by sending them his word and his spirit through chosen messengers; now, he has made himself known to the peoples of Africa by filling one of their race with his spirit and his word. It would appear that the teaching of Jehovah's Witnesses—who were very influential in Mashonaland in the 1920s and whose religious belief is much closer to the Old Testament mentality than that of the Catholic and Protestant mission churches—concerning the oneness of Jehovah God and the manner of his activity among men had found a very natural base in traditional Shona religious belief. Jehovah's Witnesses deny the full deity of Jesus Christ maintaining that Christ is 'a god' but not 'Jehovah God'. They believe that Jesus was a spirit creature called 'the word' in accordance with John 1:1 before he existed as a human being. Furthermore, they deny the personality and deity of the holy spirit which they define as 'the invisible active force of Almighty God which moves his servants to do his will' (Hoekema, 1972, 239). Such notions, therefore, are well suited to traditional Shona thought patterns.

The title most commonly applied to Johane Masowe by his followers is that of 'messenger of God to Africa'. The phrases they use are: nhume yaMwari or mutumwa waMwari (messenger of God); nhume yevatema or

---

[28] Taped extract from sermon delivered at Marrapodi, Lusaka, on 6 July, 1974. Cyprian Nedewedzo pointed out to me one very important difference between Jesus and Johane. He said that, whereas Jesus had been born with the word of God, that word had only descended on Johane when he was already grown up.

mutumwa wevatema (the messenger to black peoples); or the phrase which was inscribed on his grave, i.e., *ngirosi yeAfrica* (the angel of Africa). The Apostles, however, have also begun to apply various biblical titles to their founder, such as, 'son of God', 'son of man', 'man of God' in the sense of being a prophet, and 'god' in the sense that he is the saviour of African peoples, their messiah. Finally, a title which requires special mention, and one which is very popular among the Apostles, is that of 'the star of God'. The Shona word for 'star' is *nyenyedzi*, and it has already been noted that the falling star was traditionally regarded as a manifestation of God. The Shona word for 'lamb', on the other hand, is *nyenye*, but the lamb does not have any particular religious significance in Shona thought. It is quite significant that the Apostles have—whether by conscious intent or not—substituted the Shona word 'star' for the very similar word 'lamb' in one of their popular hymns which says, 'Star of God (the Father) which takes away the sins of the world, have mercy on us'. The phrase is taken from John 1:29 and it is most probable that Johane and his followers had heard it frequently in the mission churches. They had taken the phrase, however, and given it a more traditional and more meaningful connotation for themselves. On the other hand, the biblical symbol of the lamb as used in the Book of Revelations (14:4; 7:9–10) is often referred to by the Apostles.

In sum, then, it can be said that the manner in which the Apostles understand the role of their founder contains a unique blend of traditional and biblical religious thought patterns. Great emphasis is laid upon the person of Johane Masowe, not because of what he is, but because of what he stands for (see pp. 101–2, 113). He is the messenger who has been sent by Jehovah to African peoples just as Jesus had been sent to white peoples (as they understand it). The Apostles do not reject Jesus Christ, but they have not experienced the relevance of his work for them. The Christological controversies of the early Christian centuries do not enter into their religious awareness, and it is significant that they regard neither Jesus nor Johane Masowe as equal to God.

2. 'THE GOOD NEWS OF JOHANE MASOWE FOR AFRICA'

The only written material which the Masowe Apostles have had published is a small eight-page booklet which appeared in Nairobi, Kenya, in 1973 under the title 'The Message of God in Africa, 1932 A.D.' The content deals very briefly with the apocalyptic visions of Johane Masowe, and I have reproduced it in appendix C with the kind permission of the authors. The Apostles, however, have preserved lengthier written records of the religious experiences of their founder which comprise separate accounts. The first has been attributed to Efie, the mother of Johane Masowe; the second to Samson Mativera, the personal attendant and close friend of Johane; and the third to Onias Bvuma who was the first head-preacher to be appointed in Dewedzo and was, hence, regarded as the head-preacher of all the Apostles. I have put these three accounts together in appendix B, and they can be referred to conveniently as the Efie account (B1–17), the Mativera account (B26–36), and the Bvuma account (B37–63) respectively. A variant on the Efie account has also been included (B18–20), as well as an oral account of the signs which foretold the coming of Johane Masowe (B21–25). Two further brief accounts describe the signs and wonders which Johane Masowe performed on his arrival (B64–67 and B68–71). I have referred to the total amalgam of material mentioned above as 'The Good News of Johane Masowe for Africa' (B1–71) and it is, quite evidently, heavily influenced by biblical material, especially the Book of Revelations and the Acts of the Apostles. It is also very similar in style to 'The New Witness of the Apostles of John Maranke.' There can be little doubt but that the intention of the Apostles of Johane Masowe has been to recreate a body of material around the person of their founder which would correspond (for blacks) to that which has grown up around Jesus (for whites). It is a statement of the desire for, and reception of, a saviour or messiah by African peoples. It is a testament of faith on the part of a believing community. With the foregoing remarks in mind, then, let us consider the content of 'The Good News of Johane Masowe for Africa'.

When Efie, the mother of Shoniwa, was very young, she used to have strange dreams of white birds flying around her (B1). This was a clearly recognised visitation from God for the pigeon had come to have a symbolic value as a manifestation of the spirit with both biblical and traditional roots. This had become clear in the success which Matthew Zwimba's 'Church of the White Bird' had had in Mashonaland in the 1920s (Ranger, 1967, 38). Efie later conceived a child which kicked in her womb in a strange manner (B4) which was reminiscent of the conception of John the Baptist (Luke 1:41). This conception also bore a resemblance to Mary's visitation by an angel of God (Luke 1:26–35) for Efie also had an encounter with an angel and she conceived miraculously through the power of the holy spirit (B5–6, 18–19). Her husband had been in prison at the time and he warned her not to tell the white religious authorities in case they might interfere with the wonderful work which God had begun to accomplish for African peoples (B7, 19).

After Shoniwa had been born, he used to make strange sounds as a child and he frequently became unconscious (B8, 9, 11, 14, 20). This was a traditionally recognised sign that some spirit had wanted to take possession of him (Daneel, 1971, 131, 149). Efie was puzzled by these occurrences so she decided to take her son to a diviner-herbalist (*nganga*) to have the case diagnosed. The Efie account describes the incident as follows:

> One day, I was sitting down while he [i.e., Shoniwa] and his elder brother, Shadrech, were playing. I heard Shadrech crying and when I went to find out what was wrong, I found that my son was unconscious. His father and I went to consult a *nganga*. The *nganga* sprinkled some medicine on him three times, but each time that he did this, our son would begin to make the sounds which he used to make as a baby. The *nganga* then tried to give him some porridge mixed with medicine, but our son continued to fall unconscious. The *nganga* tried to find out the cause of these fainting fits by divining, but eventually, he admitted that he had failed. So he took up his belongings and went away. Once he had gone, my son told me that there had been a man standing beside his side while the *nganga* was trying to give him some medicine. He said that it was this man who had forbade him to take the medicine, and that he had always stood beside him whenever he fainted (B11).

The 'man' referred to above was evidently an angel of God who had forbidden Shoniwa to make use of traditional medicine. This reference to the divine prohibition of traditional medicine is a clear indication of the composition of the Efie account after the conversion experience of Johane, for he himself had mentioned in his personal statement in November 1932 that he had accepted traditional medicine during his illness (A3).

As Shoniwa began to grow up, his friends became astonished at the manner in which he was able to read for he had never gone to school (B13, 20). This was taken as a clear indication that the spirit of God had begun to take hold of him, for his knowledge could only have come from God himself. The reference to Johane's ability to read as a young man is interesting because it was clear from his frequent reading of the Bible (A5)—as well as from his ability in Port Elizabeth years later to read books in English and have passages translated into Shona for his followers—that he had become literate at a relatively early stage in his life.

The Efie account relates how a man (i.e., an angel) used to stand beside Shoniwa during his youth and how he used to tell him that one day he would have to leave home to perform the work of God—just as Jesus had had to leave his mother. When that day had arrived, he would go towards the west and return from the east (B10, 12, 16). The return from the east has both traditional and biblical connotations.

Some years, in fact, before the first appearance of Johane Masowe on the hill of Marimba, the very powers of animate and inanimate nature were believed to have proclaimed the fact that the spirit or word of God had come down upon him 'somewhere in the east':

> At midnight, there was a roar as of thunder on earth from east to west. Cattle bellowed as they looked towards the east: cocks crowed as they looked towards the east. There was noise everywhere. The noise came from the east and moved towards the west. Many people were awakened by the sound. Then the spirit (*shave*) which was in Svongosve spoke out and said that it was the word of God which had caused the noise. The spirit said that the word of God had fallen somewhere in the east (B22).

Sometime in 1932, Shoniwa had been on his way to Nyabira station near Norton by bicycle along with two friends from Nyasaland when he suddenly fell on the ground (B37). The presence of lightning is frequently referred to by the Apostles, a reference which tends to emphasise the parallel to Paul's conversion (Acts 9:3–4). His two friends from Nyasaland may well have been connected with Jehovah's Witnesses (see pp. 9–11 above), in which case their influence on Shoniwa may have been considerable. After his fall, Shoniwa had become very ill and he was taken to his hut—which his followers identify as Chipukutu's and which is referred to as such in a police file—on a European farm. Johane himself had identified the European farmer as a Mr Maitland, and the shoemaker, Jack, for whom he worked, would seem to have been the same person as Chipukutu (A3). During his illness, Shoniwa was taken care of by Chourombe Mazhambe (elsewhere identified as Saizi Sithole) and Samson Mativera. The Mativera account relates the following:

> One day when we were fast asleep, we woke up suddenly only to find that there was nobody where he [i.e., Shoniwa] had been sleeping. We heard him speaking outside the hut. We wondered how he had managed to get out, since the door was barred with the logs still in place. Outside, he was talking with Satan. The devil said to him, 'Sixpence, heaven and earth are now yours,' and he replied, 'Depart from me, Satan'. The devil said a second time, 'Sixpence, heaven and earth are now yours,' and he replied again, 'Depart from me, Satan'. Then, the devil left for a time, but he came back again later and said, 'Sixpence, heaven and earth are now yours'. He replied, 'Depart from me, Satan. Leave me alone'. Then, Satan said the same thing again, and Shoniwa made the same reply. Satan finally said, 'I have come to take away my sins. I have taken my four shillings from your side'. Sixpence replied, 'Depart from me, Satan' (B27).

Shoniwa had been known to his friends by the nickname of 'Sixpence,' and the passage above has re-created around him in an African setting the confrontation which had been described between Christ and Satan in Mt. 4:1–11. It was later explained to me that everyone born of woman was believed to have four shilings in the left side of his/her body and that this was the price of sin. The implication seems to have been that by defeating Satan, Shoniwa had been freed from the power of sin which had controlled him up to that point. This interpretation is confirmed in the passage which follows in which Shoniwa's illness is associated with the sins which he had committed. The removal of sin had now prepared him for a direct confrontation with God himself:

> He died early in the morning just before sunrise. At sunrise, we heard the voice of God calling out, 'Sixpence, Sixpence, Sixpence', three times. He replied, 'You are the Lord'. The voice of God said, 'Whom are you addressing as "Lord"?' He answered, 'Have mercy on me'. .... God then asked, 'Do you know why you have been ill for so long?' He answered, 'I don't know, Lord'. God said, 'You have been ill because of the sins which you have committed against me on earth since the day you were born. ... I want you to come back to heaven now to do my work'. He answered, 'Have mercy on me so that I may go back to the multitude on earth' (B29, 31).

The call of Sixpence three times has, undoubtedly, the call of Samuel (1 Samuel 3:8) in mind, and the number 'three' has come to have a strong symbolic significance for the Apostles. If a person swears three times, then what he says is considered to be absolutely true. If the prophets reveal something about some other person, then it has to be confirmed by two other prophets elsewhere before the prophecy can be accepted as true. The call of Shoniwa to heaven to do the work of God signifies that he had to die before he could perform this work. Once he had died to his old sinful self through baptism, he was given a new identity by God:

> Early the next morning, we heard the voice of God calling again, 'Sixpence, Sixpence, Sixpence', and his spirit answered from heaven. .... The voice then said, 'I anoint you. I now baptise you in the name of the Father and of the son and of the holy spirit, Amen. Your name is Johane. You were there in the beginning, and today you still live. Go back and tell all the people not to call you "Sixpence" any longer. They are now to call you "Baba Johane. ..." Prepare my ways until the end of the world. ... All those who will believe in you will have everlasting joy. Whatever you say there on earth, I will be listening to here in heaven' (B34).

The influence of Mk. 16:16 and John 20:23 is clear in the passage above in which Christ commissioned his disciples to carry on his work by giving them the power of his spirit.

The Apostles really do believe that their founder did die and rise again as a new person and with a new mission. They make a strong point of the fact that Shoniwa's European employer came to verify his death (B39), a testimony which is repeated many times. The Bvuma account claims that the European had sent workmen to bury Shoniwa, but that, as they had not been able to complete the burial in one day, they had just left the coffin in the grave and had covered it over with a sheet of asbestos intending to finish filling in the grave on the following day (B39). Various versions of this incident give different reasons as to why the grave had not been filled in, such as that darkness had fallen too soon, that the ground was too hard and the sun was too hot, or that the rain had begun to fall heavily. At any rate, when the workmen returned the following morning, the grave was empty (B40) just as in John 20:1.

Shoniwa was later on discovered on the hill of Marimba singing the song 'Hosanna' (B40), having in his possession a staff and a Bible, and wearing a white garment (B51) which is described as 'seamless' in accordance with Jn. 19:23. These three objects (i.e., the white garment, the staff and the Bible) were believed to have been given to Johane in a miraculous manner and the staff itself was also supposed to have sung 'Hosanna'. The Apostles who had accompanied me to the hill of Marimba told me that it was a tree which used to sing 'Hosanna' and they showed me the dead trunk of the tree (see fig. 5). The three objects

FIG. 5. Apostles beside trunk of 'singing tree' on Marimba Hill, Rhodesia.

mentioned above are the standard equipment of a religious prophet and are considered to be very important in establishing the authenticity of a prophet's work. Johane himself, however, had clearly acknowledged the human source of these objects (A5–6).

While Johane was preaching on the hill of Marimba, the European was once again called to verify the fact that he had risen from the dead (B40). The European asked Johane—who is, in fact, referred to by his baptismal name, Peter, here—how it had come about that he had died and risen again. Johane replied:

> When you put me in the grave, I saw a man who came from heaven. This man carried me up, and we went into heaven. He took me to the first gate. I saw a man who had been sitting down and he told me that his name was Abraham. He opened the gate for me. At the second gate, there was a man called Isaac, and at the third gate, a man called Jacob. While I was at this gate, I heard the sound of thunder on the inside. I also heard much complaining and I trembled through fear (B41).

The Bvuma account makes it quite clear that the God who had sent his angel to bring Johane to heaven was Jehovah, the God of Abraham, Isaac and Jacob. It was on to this line of salvation history that Johane—and through him, all the African races—was being grafted; and it was the spirit of the God which had been at work in the line of Shem which was now being given to Johane and to the line of Ham (to which all the black races were believed to belong).

In traditional Shona society, the carrying out of abortions and the killing of twins or deformed babies was not uncommon,[29] and the complaints which Johane had heard at the third gate of heaven came from just such victims. They blamed witches (*varoyi*) for their fate and were anxious that God might bring the world to an end so that those who were guilty might be brought to justice (B43–44). Jesus, however, had appeared on the scene and had reassured them that he was going to initiate a new plan of salvation for African peoples before the world would be brought to an end. He took Johane's hand and brought him to the river. The account continues:

> At this point, Jesus baptised Johane. Johane put his right leg into the water and, when he took it out, it was white. The whole of his right side became white. The left side still remained black, as black as people on earth [i.e., the peoples of Africa]. Johane asked what was the meaning of one side becoming white and the other remaining black. He was told, 'The black side means that if holy ones arrive [in heaven], they will be sent back to

[29] See Charles Bullock (1927), p. 273; Daneel (1971), p. 312; Gelfand (1973), p. 171. Cf. Rev. 6:10–11 and the Book of Enoch, chapter nine.

earth'. Johane then said that he would go back to earth because the world was evil (B45).

This type of symbolic reference to salvation for peoples of different colours is very common among African prophets. George Khambule used to say that he had seen Jesus in one of his visions as half white and half black, and Isaiah Shembe used to say, 'I am of all colours.' (Becken, 1965, 103). The point being made in the passage above is that, since African peoples had not yet received their saviour through whom they could be properly baptised, they were blocked from entering heaven. Johane, however, was now going to return to earth to remedy the situation.

The Bvuma account continues by describing the encounters which took place between Johane and the white political and religious authorities in Southern Rhodesia. The latter are portrayed as powers which attempted to prevent Johane from fulfilling his new mission. It is important to note here that his struggle is portrayed as primarily against the evils of traditional Shona society. His goal is to destroy witches and all that is connected with them and to bring his people the saving power of baptism. His struggle is only against the white political and religious powers in so far as they have either failed to help his own people or are attempting to prevent him from saving them from evil. The fact that God is on Johane's side is emphasised by the fact that, like Peter in Acts 12:6–17, an angel is sent to him to release him from prison miraculously (B54). His white garment, staff and Bible are taken from him because the white powers know that his new power rests in these objects (B54, 63). In the manner of John the Baptist, he continues to live on locusts and honey (B55). Johane's confrontation with the political authorities is described as follows:

> I stood in the witness box and they asked me who I was. I replied, 'I am John the Baptist'. But they said, 'You are Shoniwa'. I agreed and said, 'That was my name a long time ago. Now, I am John the Baptist. I was sent as a messenger to the Africans. This is the name which is inherited by messengers whether they be Africans or Whites. I was once sent to Judaea as a white messenger, but now here in Rhodesia, I am a messenger to the black people. In God's language, 'Johane' means 'a new beginner' or 'the beginner of new things'. I am making a new way amongst black people. Our fathers never learnt this way (B55).

The white authorities insist that the white churches have told them that Jesus is 'the new way', and that they have been taught 'to pray, to be good people, and to be baptised' (B56). Johane points out, however, that if they had carried out God's instructions in regard to the African people, there would not have been any need for him to perform his special work (B56).

Shortly afterwards, the representatives of the established mission churches assemble together to question Johane and they ask him what kind of a teacher he is. He replies:

> I am a teacher of the whole world. I am saying that people should stop practising witchcraft, throw away their medicines (makona), pray to God, and love one another. Throw away harmful medicines (nyanga) because the world is coming to an end (B59).

He then proceeds to criticise the mission churches for their failure to send their ministers among Africans in the reserves and in the towns. Furthermore, he accuses them of doing wrong by associating with witches who have been responsible for the premature deaths of innocent children (B60). He refuses to allow the priests to build a church for him because this would restrict the scope of his work saying, 'My church is the wilderness. This means that the whole world is my church' (B61). This latter criticism seems to imply that the white missionaries were not really encountering Africans on a meaningful level within the confines of the walls of a church. What God had wanted was that they should bring the true religion to Africans in their home environment where it really mattered.

The twofold confrontation with the white authorities mentioned above paints a clear picture of the climate within which Johane Masowe had begun his work. His work was on behalf of black people whereas their concern was considered to be for white people. He had come with the power of John the Baptist to get black people to repent and to discard their evil ways; he had come with the spirit of Jesus to baptise them so that they might be enabled to enter into heaven. There was no time to waste for the world would soon come to an end. The white authorities might try to prevent him from carrying out his task by beating him (B63) but nothing would stop him from fulfilling his God-given mission.

3. THE BIBLE AS THE WORD OF GOD FOR AFRICA

It has already been noted that Johane Masowe had a very strong personal devotion to the Bible (i.e. the New Testament as well as the Old Testament) which he used to read frequently. When he first appeared on the hill of Marimba, one of the sacred objects which he had in his possession was a Bible. At first, however, his followers did not identify it as an ordinary Bible for it had been given to Johane by God in order to carry out his mission among Africans only. Johane had, in fact, encouraged his followers to throw away their Bibles which had become too closely associated with the white Christ and the white mission churches. The Book which he himself had brought with him was the special word of God for Africa. Only he, as the lawfully appointed messenger of God, was in a position to interpret the meaning of this Book. Indeed, Johane himself *was* the word of God for Africa and, by listening to him, African peoples would learn what God wanted them to do.

It would appear, however, that once Johane had begun to appoint preachers to help him, the need of using the Bible had arisen. African preachers from other religious bodies were using it, and the followers of Johane had become embarrassed about not having any acceptable written justification for their preaching. Due to their persuasion, Johane reluctantly—according to evangelist Nedewedzo—allowed them to make use of the Bible. He made it clear, however, that its use would remain subject to his interpretation. Only he, as the embodiment of the word of God, would be capable of reading it properly for African peoples. Years later, when the Apostles had begun to make a more serious study of the Bible by using various kinds of biblical commentaries, Johane himself carefully selected those passages which, he insisted, were meant for Africa. As the years passed, however, the Apostles began to identify the Bible more and more with what their founder was saying. Today, it has become accepted as the word of Johane Masowe who himself is the word of God for Africa. The following extract has been taken from a sermon which was delivered by an Apostle at Marrapodi, Lusaka, in July 1974:

> When the 'son of man' (*mwana wamunhu*) came to us, he said these things whilst we were at the sea [i.e., at Port Elizabeth]. He explained the Bible adding to what had been said by Our Lord because Baba Johane came wearing a white garment which was referred to in the Bible. On account of this, we were convinced. We left our mothers and we left our relations knowing that we had found what we had been seeking in the Wesley church and in various other churches. We saw that what Baba Johane did conformed with the Bible. I'm thankful and happy because we are in the word of God. There is nothing which we seek outside the Bible. If you seek something outside the Bible, then it is your own fault. You are the one who will be doing things which are against the commandments. ... The way in which we should pray is in the books [of the Bible], and all the sayings [i.e., of Baba Johane] are in the verses. We see them all [in practice] among those who pray. ... Be careful, you who look for the words of Baba Johane outside the Bible. ... You should not go and seek the word of God in the darkness for we have the word of God with us. We used to pass greetings with him saying, 'Good morning, Lord', and he would reply, 'I've come among you, the children of Africa, with the word of God'. What is the meaning of all this? It means this: Africa, wake up and

get down the mountain, because you have the word of God among you.
Every song that you sing, you sing in the word of God; everywhere you go,
you must know that you go in the word of God; whatever work you do,
you do in the word of God. You should not read, then, outside the Bible.
What is it that you seek which is not written there? It is what is written in
the verses of the Bible that really matters.

The passage above emphasises the attitude of the Apostles, not just
towards the Bible but towards secular education as well (see pp. 122–23
below). The latter can only have value if acquired for the sake of understanding the Bible more fully.

In the early days of his preaching, Johane Masowe had been very
critical of the failure of the mission churches. Later on, however, when
his own position had become more firmly established, he had begun to
praise the white mission churches for preparing those who were to
become his followers. He expressed this by saying that the established
white churches had familiarised his followers with his word before he
had come in person to lead them.

In traditional Shona religious belief, it was very important for an
individual to share in the ancestral spirit (*mudzimu*) of his grandfather
during his lifetime. After his death, his own spirit would then receive
an individuality of its own and, in time, he might even enter the ranks
of the tribal ancestral spirits as a *mhondoro* (Murphree, 1969, 33–4;
Daneel, 1971, 96–8). In the case of Johane Masowe, his followers
believe that the spirit of Jesus had taken hold of him during his life.
Now that he has died, however, he is believed to have attained the
status of a tribal ancestral spirit like Chaminuka in traditional Shona
belief or (as the Apostles believe) like Jesus in Christian belief. Just as
Jesus is believed to be the father of salvation history for the Jews and
for the white races—and belongs to the same ancestral line of Shem as
Abraham, Isaac and Jacob—so Johane has now become the father of
salvation history for African peoples; and the ancestral line of Ham
has been grafted on the line of Shem by receiving the spirit of Jesus
who was the last of the prophets sent to the Jews. Johane is, indeed (as
a Masowe preacher put it) 'the last saviour of the last church' for the
peoples of Africa. In the words of evangelist Cyprian Nedewedzo:

> Throughout the whole of Africa and among all African peoples, the light
> had not shone in Africa right from the time of Adam onwards and we
> never had a prophet of our own. When Noah came, he left Africans out-
> side of his ark. Our forefather, Ham, was cursed by Noah so that he might
> become the slave of slaves. . . . When Moses was sent to lead the Israelites
> from Egypt into Canaan, he was told not to have mercy on the people
> whom he found there. . . . When Jesus came, he was asked why he had
> come, and he said that he had come for the lost sheep of Israel. The race of

Ham was neglected once again, and so, it did not obey the commandments. . . . In 1932, the word of God came and made it clear that it
had come to the race of Ham. We received this word with great joy,
because we knew that God had begun to visit the peoples of Africa.

The Apostles interpret the Bible in a very literalistic and fundamentalistic manner and they have little difficulty in finding themselves and
their history outlined in prophecy in its pages. It had been foretold in
Zep. 3:9–10 that Jehovah would give to his people a pure tongue with
which to sing to him, and that the daughter of his scattered ones would
come from the region of the rivers of Ethiopia. Two of these rivers
were called Pishon and Gihon, the first surrounding the country of
Havilah, the second, that of Cush (Gen. 2:11). It is evident to the
Apostles that the rivers Pishon and Gihon refer to the rivers Zambezi
and Nile respectively, and that the countries of Havilah and Cush refer
likewise to Rhodesia and Ethiopia respectively. It is equally clear to the
Apostles that the country of Havilah (i.e., Rhodesia)—from which
much gold came—is the country referred to in 2 Chron. 9:10 in which
Ophir is mentioned, for Ophir is the origin of the word 'Fur' (Fura)
which, in turn, is the Shona name for the present Mount Darwin in
Rhodesia. It is also clear to the Apostles that the prophet Enoch was
referring to Rhodesia when he foretold that the Most High, the New
Jerusalem, would descend in the land of the south (see Enoch 77:2;
90:28–29).

The Apostles have adopted the Hebrew word 'messiah' to refer to
their founder as their saviour. When I asked evangelist Jordan
Chikorosa if there were more than one messiah, he answered, 'There
can be many messiahs. Jesus Christ was the messiah for the Europeans
just as Baba Johane is the messiah for the Africans. Anyone who is sent
by God is a messiah'. Evangelist Ernest Maposa expanded on this idea
at another time:

Jesus came at his own time. He preached to many people including the
Apostles, and they were converted. He lived with them until the time of his
death. Before he died, however, he had said to them, 'I am going away,
but I will not leave you alone. I will send you the holy spirit to stay with
you'. After Jesus had died, the Apostles went to assemble in Jerusalem
where the spirit which had been promised came down upon them. Then,
they went out everywhere preaching the gospel, praying for the sick and
healing them and performing all kinds of wonders. They continued to do
this until they died. For this reason, Isaiah prophesied that the messiah
would come in the end [i.e., in the last days]. It was prophesied that the
messiah would come to the Africans in a place south of the Zambezi on
Mount Darwin.

The Apostles believe, then, that Johane Masowe came to bring them
the saving power of Jesus so that they might bring it to their own people. The Bible, as the word of God, had not only foretold this, but it
has given clear directives as to how the Apostles should continue to live
their new way of life.[30]

4. THE ROLE-IDENTITY OF THE SPIRITUAL 'WIVES' OF JOHANE MASOWE

Shortly after Johane Masowe had settled with some of his followers in
Port Elizabeth, he had sent his evangelists back to Southern Rhodesia
to search for chosen 'boys' and 'girls' who would dedicate themselves
to serving him. The duty of the 'boys' would be to work in order to
earn money for church requirements, as well as to provide food for the
'girls'. The duty of the 'girls' would be to do the work of God by
singing at Jordans [i.e., baptisms] and by praying for the freedom of
Africa. These evangelists, according to Cyprian Nedewedzo, had been
told to say to parents:

---

[30] Masowe prayer-services, which I had recorded over a period of three months, revealed that
the Apostles had drawn on a wide range of texts from all over the Bible. Forty texts from the Old
Testament (plus one from the Book of Enoch) were commented upon as compared with thirty-
eight texts from the New Testament. The topics dealt with most frequently were: (1) apocalyptic
themes and themes dealing with the last judgment, (2) the Apostles as the elect of God in Africa,
(3) moralistic themes dealing with the observance of the Sabbath, obeying the laws of God, financial contributions, and giving an example of good behaviour, and (4) spreading the gospel
message throughout Africa.

Ever since the Masowe Apostles first settled in Port Elizabeth they have continued to collect
and use a wide selection of Bible Concordances and Commentaries. Apocryphal literature is pop-
ular and I have seen numerous copies of the *Book of Enoch*, the *Books of Esther* and the *Book of the
Assumption of Moses* at Marrapodi as well as two copies of the two volumes of R. H. Charles, *The
Apocrypha and Pseudepigrapha of the Old Testament* (OUP, Ely House, London, first published 1913).
Other works which I have seen among the Apostles both in Lusaka and Nairobi are: *The Book of
Legends: Tales from the Talmud and Midrash* (New York: Hebrew Publishing Company, 1929); *The
Bible Story*, Vol. 1, Arthur S. Maxwell (Review and Herald Publishing Association, Washington,
D.C., 1954); *Legends of the Bible*, 7 vols, Louis Ginzberg (Jewish Publication Society of America,
Simon & Schuster, Inc., New York, 1909, 1910, 1911, 1913, 1956); *The Messianic Idea in Israel*,
Joseph Klausner, Ph.D. (translated from 3rd Hebrew edition by W. F. Stinespring, Macmillan
Co., New York, 1955); *Dispensational Truth or God's Plan and Purpose in the Ages*, Clarence Larkin,
publ. by Clarence Larkin Est., 2802 N. Park Ave., Philadelphia, Pa., U.S.A. Two items in par-
ticular which were circulating freely among the Apostles in mimeographed form were translations
into Shona of many selections from the *Torah* applied in fundamentalistic fashion to the coming
of Johane, the Messiah, in Rhodesia as well as a lengthy continuous selection entitled
'Constitutions of the Holy Apostles' which was taken from *The Ante-Nicene Fathers*, Vol. 7, pp.
391–405 (translations of 'The Writings of the Fathers' down to A.D. 325 by the Rev. Alexander
Roberts, D.D. and James Donaldson, LL.D. editors—American reprint of the Edinburgh edition
revised and chronologically arranged by A. Cleveland Coxe, D.D.—W. B. Eerdmans Publishing Co.,
Michigan: Grand Rapids).

Whoever gives up a child, so that he or she may always be praying, will receive life. Even in the beginning, there were 'boys' and 'girls' living with the men at Jerusalem. The same thing applies now to this generation. This group must live here now, because it is this group which will survive until the time when God will be reigning.

The biblical framework within which this appeal had been made was also based on Shona traditional religious beliefs. In the days of the Rozvi kings, it was customary for Shona chiefs to demonstrate their loyalty to *Mwari* by dedicating their sons and daughters to his service (Daneel, 1970, 26). These junior male and female priests, these 'children of God,' were known as *hosannahs* (*sic*) and *mbonga* respectively, and they were subjected to 'special taboos concerning the use of food and their relation to the opposite sex' (Daneel, 1970, 49). The *mbongas* used to assist the *mbonga-svikiro* who acted as the voice of God within the cave (see p. 47 above). It had also become customary for Shona parents in general to dedicate their daughters to *Mwari* who then came to be regarded as 'wives' of *Mwari* (Daneel, 1971, 86). The use of the term 'wives' in this spiritual sense expressed the nature of the total dedication of these girls to *Mwari*. Once they had reached marriageable age, it was up to *Mwari* to decide on their future (Daneel, 1970, 49). It is not quite clear whether or not they automatically became the actual wives of the officiating priests (Daneel, 1971, 85, n.16).[31] The traditional basis for girls living of chastity was found not only in the cult of *Mwari* but in the *mhondoro* ancestral cult as well. Gelfand states that

> ... the *masvikiro* of Dotito were given wives who had to live in chastity apart from other people. No one dare tamper with these wives of Nyanhehwe and the other *mhondoro*, for if discovered, the guilty person would be burnt at the stake (1962, 28).

Almost from the very beginning of his preaching ministry, Johane had insisted on the need for girls who would accompany him in his travels, and who would sing during baptisms. When he had moved from Mashonaland to Matabeleland at the end of the 1930s, he had sent his evangelists back to Mashonaland to request that parents might allow some of their children to come and serve him. In Bulawayo, he had already begun the process of training them in a special way, but it was only when he had settled in Port Elizabeth that he had succeeded in organising the way of life of these girls on a more stable basis. It would

[31] Although the actual history of the *Mwari* cult remains somewhat uncertain, the practice of dedicating boys and girls to the service of the cult centres is carried on today. The dedicated persons leave later on, often as more senior religious functionaries such as spirit mediums or cult messengers, and usually marry.

appear that many parents did respond to the request of Johane to send their sons and daughters to Port Elizabeth, although many were reluctant to do so on account of the distance involved. At first, the girls lived in different houses, but later on Johane had insisted that they all live together. By this time, they had come to be referred to as the 'wives' of *Baba* Johane (Father John). It is worth noting that by then, Johane had already married six wives although three had died. The other 'wives' were looked upon as spiritual ones on account of their dedication to his service. When these 'wives' reached marriageable age, Johane reluctantly allowed some of them to get married to some of the 'boys' who had also become dedicated to his service (see p. 109 below). He encouraged others, however, never to get married.

As the number of followers attracted by Johane's message had continued to grow, and as new congregations had begun to spring up in places very far apart, it had become necessary for Johane to appoint prophets, preachers and evangelists to help him with his work (see chapter V, pp. 102–8 below). Greater organisation had become necessary if the initial impact of his message was not to perish. The institutionalisation of the 'wives' of Baba Johane had begun to play a prominent role in this respect. These 'wives' had slowly begun to lose their importance as mere individuals and had begun to take on a collective symbolic value which represented the presence of God himself in their midst. In a sense, they had taken on an importance and a significance which was even greater than that of the person of Johane. Johane, like Moses, had been given the privileged mission of leading the people of God to the Promised Land; but it was his 'wives' who had come to represent the carrier of God's presence among them. Under the growing influence of biblical symbolism and imagery, the 'wives' had become the ark of the covenant, the house of God, the guarantee of the saved remnant.

During the years spent in Port Elizabeth, Johane Masowe had actually begun to build a small ship, a ship which he believed would save the chosen people on the day of the great destruction. From 1932 onwards, he had continued to believe that the end of the world was near and, like Noah, he had begun to prepare for that day. Some years later, the following was reported in a Salisbury newspaper:

> They [i.e., the Basketmakers] were constantly repairing an ark which took them years to build and which they say will carry them to New Jerusalem (*Daily News*, 6.6.62).[32]

[32] Some of the Apostles have told me that Baba Johane had first insisted on building a boat in imitation of Noah and in preparation for the destruction of the world. But he also had in mind the idea of travelling by sea as far as Jerusalem. Gradually, however, he began to think more in

Under the influence of a growing knowledge of the Bible, the notion of the saving ark was accompanied by the notion of the box of wood in which the presence of God would remain among his wandering people. It is most probable that this shift in emphasis from the ship to the box developed at the time when the Apostles realised that they would not be allowed to remain in Port Elizabeth. It would now be necessary to carry their saving ark with them. By this time, Johane had already been thinking in terms of his 'wives' representing the presence of God on account of their purity in abstaining from sexual relations. Consequently, he had begun to think of them more and more as the 'ark of God' and as 'mothers of the covenant'. The following has been preserved in English at Nairobi in the written records of the Apostles:

> As regarding the ark of virgins, Father John declared that he had been advised by God to set it up, for it is a covenant between God and his world. Adding, he said, that if the ark lasts up till the great and dreadful day of the Lord, the believers shall escape the destruction to come just as it was in the days of Noah when eight souls were rescued through the ark. He enjoined the damsels to adhere to chastity and purity till they die.

The saving ark had by then been transformed from an ark of wood into an ark of human beings. The 'wives' of *Baba* Johane had taken on a role of crucial significance, a role which indicated a major development in the religious belief of the Masowe Apostles. These 'wives' are frequently referred to today as 'Sisters' by those living close to them, but this term (chosen because of the presumed similar lifestyle with religious Sisters in established churches) is not generally recognised among Apostles in the rural areas.

After the Apostles had been deported from South Africa, they made their new headquarters in Lusaka, Zambia. The Sisters (as I shall refer to them from now on) also settled there. In fact, it had come to be understood that wherever the Sisters were, there would be the headquarters. There is a large fig tree (*mukuyu*) in Marrapodi compound in Lusaka which, the Apostles believe, marked the spot around which their founder had foretold that they would settle (see fig. 3, p. 39 above). In 1963, Johane himself visited the Apostles there and spoke to a very large crowd which had gathered around this fig tree. He spoke,

---

terms of moving up through Africa and the emphasis shifted from building a ship to building a coach (or bus) which would transport his 'wives' by land. Fr Adrian Hastings has kindly brought to my attention an article which appeared in the *Observer* in 1955 on the Masowe community in Port Elizabeth in which was written: '. . . like Noah, they are building an Ark to travel in when the time comes. It is not, of course, a ship. It is a motor-coach and promises to be one with unusually solid and imposing bodywork. On its windows the Sabbatarians have engraved the symbol of their Church—a seven-branched candlestick set on the summit of the world.' See Cyril Dunn, 'Black Christians Build an Ark,' *Observer*, June 26, 1955, p. 13.

in particular, about the Sisters and their central importance for all believers as well as for the development and expansion of his mission. On that day, (a Masowe preacher exclaimed) he had said:

> This house is the salvation of Africa. It is the one to be prayed to. It is the one which will save Africa because they are the singers who are singing for Africa so that it may be saved.

'This house' is a term which is often applied to the Sisters, and it seems to have a twofold connotation: the first, with reference to the Sisters as the 'wives of the big house', an expression which indicates the importance of their relationship to Johane himself in a traditional manner; the second, with reference to God's choice of the house of Ham to which the African races belong. The Sisters are thought to represent the whole house of Ham in the collective symbolic sense of a corporate personality, and all those who remain in union with the Sisters are included among the saved. Johane himself had made it quite clear that prayers to God should be addressed through this house and not through him. A Masowe preacher quoted him as saying: 'This house is the one which should be prayed to. Don't pray facing me.' The Sisters

FIG. 6. Sisters at Nairobi, Kenya, with Head Sister, Meggi Matanhire, holding book.

have a role to play as mediatrix between God and man; and the effectiveness of the preaching of the Apostles depends on the preservation of the Sisters. Johane had emphasised this (said another Masowe preacher) when speaking at the *mukuyu* tree:

> This is the covenant I want to make with these Sisters. With Moses, there was the ark of wood; today, your ark is to be the Sisters. Everybody should pray facing it. Your prayers should pass through it [lit., 'walk through it'].
> ... Wherever you may go to preach the gospel, you must look after this house, because this is where God is present [lit., 'where God stands'].

When Johane had become ill in Tanzania, some of the Sisters had remained with him, and in 1972, they had moved to Nairobi in Kenya with him. At present, an attempt is being made to have all the Sisters living together there (see pp. 108–9 below). Nairobi holds a very special significance for the Apostles, for they believe that it is in the middle of Africa. One of the Bible texts which has become very precious to them is Isaiah 19:19 which makes reference to the altar which is to be erected to Jehovah in the midst of Egypt. Since Egypt symbolises Africa for the Apostles, they understand the altar to be a clear reference to the fact that the Sisters are intended by God to be established there. They also refer to the temple which is to be built at Nairobi, but when I asked one of the Sisters concerning this temple building, she said: 'No. No temple building is going to be built for *Baba* Johane. We, the Sisters, are the temple. Wherever the Sisters are, there is the temple.' On the other hand, the dwelling place of Johane both in Port Elizabeth and in Lusaka was referred to by the Apostles as 'the temple'. Johane Masowe himself is spoken of as the temple in Jerusalem described in the Book of Enoch 90:28–31 which was carried away to the land of the south (i.e., Rhodesia) where it will be rebuilt as the New Jerusalem (see Rev. 11:19). The fact that the Sisters are also referred to as the New Jerusalem suggests a form of identity between themselves and Johane, an identity which is explained in terms of the identical roles which they are both understood to play. The Sisters have now become 'the holy city, New Jerusalem, coming down out of heaven from God and prepared as a bride adorned for her husband' (Rev. 21:2).

Exactly one year after the death of Johane Masowe, his loyalist followers gathered at Gandanzara to hold their first universal Synod and to complete the burial rites of their founder (see p. 42 above). The presence of some Sisters was vital for the successful accomplishment of the latter. After they had knelt around the grave, they said aloud:

> We, your handmaids, have come. On the day of your sleeping, we were

not able to do what we ought to have done. Today, however, we have come to anoint your body. All your family is beseeching you that you may not leave us alone.[33]

The Sisters then wiped the top of the grave clean with their hands without using brushes, and the senior Sister present addressed the elders as follows:

We have some oils which *Baba* Johane gave us to keep a long time ago. The oils were bought in Jerusalem and were given to us while we were still in Baai [i.e., Port Elizabeth]. The oils are from the olive tree. *Baba* Johane gave us instructions concerning these oils that, if anything should happen to him, we were to smear his body with them.[34]

When she had said this, she began to sprinkle the oils over the top of the grave while the other Sisters sang the hymn, 'Star of God the Father'. Then, she took a white cloth and spread it out over the grave saying: 'This is our covering of *Baba* today because we were prevented from doing this by the breakaway group'.

While the ritual as described above is placed within a traditional framework, the influence of the Bible narrative concerning the burial of Jesus is unmistakeable (see John 12:7 and John 19:40).

Apart from settling the spirit of the deceased, the traditional Shona *kugadzira* ritual also included the question of the succession to the deceased's name, and the disposal of the deceased's inheritable wives and property (Daneel, 1971, 101–103; Gelfand, 1959, 203). It was a traditional Shona custom that the eldest brother in the family of the deceased would be the one to inherit wives and property. Johane, however, had emphasised to his followers again and again that, ever since his rebirth and acquisition of a new identity, he was no longer a member of his natural family. His new family was based on spiritual bonds. In practice, however, this is only true in regard to Johane's more immediate relations for, while none of his brothers has been given any position of importance, members of his extended family have wielded great power right from the start (see p. 19 above). The Sisters, as his spiritual 'wives', were to be inherited by the leaders of the church, viz., the evangelists. Indeed, Johane used to say in Port Elizabeth that the evangelists were his younger brothers. The following record of an exhortation which he gave to the Sisters has been preserved by the Apostles:

Vadzimai ('wives' or mothers), if anything happens to me, you should not get married or be inherited by Shedrech [i.e. his elder brother] and his

---

[33] Extract from report on Synod drawn up by an Apostle.
[34] Ibid.

young brothers. No one can succeed me, not even my children. My kingdom is not of this world. This kingdom of heaven is of the love of God, and my spirit cannot be put to rest (*kugadzirwa*) by the thoughts and love of men. It is from God alone. *Vadzimai*, if anything should ever happen to me, you should not leave this place. You will see the glory of God in the future. Miracles and wonders will take place. Amen.

As the final burial rites of Johane Masowe took place, his loyalist followers were quite clear about their founder's intentions.

When the Synod had come to an end, the Apostles were filled with a firm conviction that their founder had not left them for his spirit had still remained on actively among them. This spirit was to be found at work in three places in particular, viz., in the supreme council of seventy which had been decided upon, in the body of law which Johane had left to his followers, and in the collective body of the Sisters. The three, however, would have to be working in harmony if the true spirit of Johane were to be recognised. The Synod re-confirmed the essential mission of their founder, namely, to continue spreading the gospel message of salvation throughout Africa and to tend towards Jerusalem. This apostolic thrust had always been the central point and key factor of Johane's mission, and his followers have not lost it (see pp. 99–108 below).

5. PRAYERS AND HYMNS AMONG THE APOSTLES

An attempt has been made in the foregoing pages to express some of the implicit doctrinal elements of religious belief among the Masowe Apostles. So far, of course, the Apostles have not formulated their religious beliefs within any clear doctrinal framework. On the other hand, certain features of their present belief system stand out very clearly. The following can be mentioned in particular: their founder-prophet, Johane Masowe, has been sent to them as the saviour of the black races; he plays the same role for the black races as Jesus played for the white races, for the same spirit of God is present in both; the God who has chosen the African races of the line of Ham is Jehovah, the God of the Bible; hence, the Bible has become the new charter in which the course of the Apostles as the new Israelites has already been plotted; the Sisters have a crucial role to play in keeping alive the spirit of Johane; the mission entrusted to the Apostles by Jehovah through their prophet is that of proclaiming the message of salvation, first to African peoples and then to all peoples, before the end should come; and the goal of their mission is to reach Jerusalem so that the New Jerusalem may renovate the earth.

Apart from the oral tradition which has been passed on among the Apostles, the documents which they have preserved in written form, and the sermons which are preached during Sabbath services, one of the most reliable methods of evaluating the religious beliefs of a people is through their personal prayers and the hymns which they sing. The former tend to express these beliefs in a more spontaneous fashion, the latter in a more formal and stereotyped fashion. What follows, then, is a short selection of extracts from personal prayers and hymns of the Apostles which were recorded in 1974 during prayer-services at Marrapodi, Lusaka. No further attempt will be made here to expand on their content, but it will be clear that they reinforce the religious beliefs mentioned above.

(i) Personal prayers (a selection)

1. Alleluia. In your name, Father, the son and the holy spirit. We thank you, the God of *Baba* Johane. ... You have given us your commandments, Father. We went to the sea [i.e. to Port Elizabeth] to build your church there. ... Listen, your servants are now speaking. Your 'house' is here along with the evangelists, the prophets, the preachers, and the 'teachers'. The whole church has assembled here to pray. Alleluia.

2. Almighty God, powerful Jehovah, the worker of miracles, you were at mount Marimba singing 'Hosanna'. All those in their homes, and even the beasts of the forest, heard you. Everyone came when they heard the way you sang 'Hosanna'. You ruled the whole land, Father. You travelled on foot. They heard your word, Jehovah. Listen to the prayers of your people, the ones you have chosen here on earth who have assembled here. We are no longer of the earth since you have chosen us from the earth. Your seed has gathered here today.

3. Your people have assembled, Jehovah. They are glorifying your name, Jehovah, our saviour. ... You sent *Baba* Johane, our father [in faith] to our fathers, Jehovah. ... Listen to our prayers, God of Israel.

4. We are praying to you, the holy one who descended on earth. You, the spirit of heaven, have come from heaven and have descended on earth. You have lived in the body of someone born on earth.

5. You descended on mount Marimba, Father, to fulfil the prophecy of Enoch. It was said that you would descend in the last days in the land of the south. You came to fulfil the promise to Africa. ... It was said that he shall descend. One shall descend and call out in a loud voice in the lands of Africa. It is said that he shall be followed by leaders and by a congregation of thousands upon thousands, an uncountable number garbed in white. ... We thank you, Jehovah, the father of Abraham ... you sent the holy spirit. ... We thank you, Father, the God of Africa, the God of *Baba* Johane. ... The 'son of God' called out from mount Marimba standing close to a tree. He stood in the middle of the tree of

life calling out in a loud voice, 'Let Hosanna come; let Africa be saved'.
. . . Let your love spread throughout Africa so that Africa may be
blessed and that it may be freed from its troubles. . . . The light
descended on mount Marimba. It came calling out to Africa saying, 'I
want girls who will sing for Africa so that Africa may be saved'. May the
words of the holy be fulfilled in 'this house'. . . . *Baba* Johane took the
'girls of Africa' so that they might pray for Africa. May the mercy of
God remain in Africa.

6. In those days, Father, we came as sinners and we fell down and confessed our sins. You baptised us in the river Jordan. It was this that
saved the children of men on earth. . . . Father, you visited many places
spreading the gospel of your kingdom. The spirits of the earth came
out and they shook. Hands were placed on the heads of the sick and
they were healed. . . . Jehovah, you baptised with water and with the
blood of the holy spirit. People believed because they saw that it was
written in the Bible. . . . May we carry your good words and spread
them among all nations.

7. God the Father, we thank you. . . . Those who are here, and those who
are at the four corners of the world, went to hear your word. They are
awaiting all the time to hear about your kingdom. May those who are
with us at this time be blessed. We are looking for those others so that
we may bring them to you. . . . May your name be respected and sanc-
tified throughout the whole world. Let it be known that you are God in
those lands where your word has not reached yet. Let it be known that
you came to save the children of Africa who have been oppressed by the
great darkness.

8. You are the one who sent *Baba* Johane. The holy spirit descended at
Pentecost. It filled the whole world and all the people heard it. All the
people who were there, and all the Apostles who were there, were happy to proclaim the name of Jesus because the spirit had demonstrated
his works. Therefore, God of heaven, I believe that these people are
here because of your spirit which you sent to your prophet. You gave
'Hosanna' [i.e. *Baba* Johane] the work to do, and he went about
spreading your word.

(ii) Hymns (a selection)

1. Let Jehovah conquer in the whole of Africa
   As he did at Jersusalem.
2. May Jehovah send (a messenger) to Africa.
3. We thank him who came to Africa.
4. Lord, guide the Apostles.
5. The light has come into this country.
6. Now it is our turn to take your word to those outside; they don't know
   Our Lord. . . .
   Let us go, friends, to the harvest field of believers which is given for

ploughing in order to conquer the wicked.

7. God our Father who is in heaven, stay with your servants in this land. Those who love you will do the work of heaven.

8. Star of God (the Father), which takes away the sins of the world, have mercy on us.

9. Greetings, Jesus, you have come today: may you stay with us; may we stay with you.

10. The word descended from heaven. It spoke to the Apostles. It wanted to go down to Babylon.

11. Come, spirit.

The religious belief of the Masowe Apostles has undergone a gradual process of change and development since 1932, a process which has tended to become more and more dependent on a biblical framework. So far, the Apostles' use of the Bible has tended to be very fundamentalistic, and a dialectic interaction has been taking place between their understanding of events in their own history, and those related of the Israelites in the Bible. The influence of Watch Tower teaching of an apocalyptic and literalistic type has tended to be very dominant in their interpretation of the Bible, but in recent years, they have shown signs of greater flexibility. At present, they are very anxious that their ministers should receive a more thorough training in Bible study, and their future religious development may well depend on the outcome of such measures. Since the death of Johane Masowe, a tragedy which has been heightened by the split among themselves, the loyalist Apostles have been forced to reflect more consciously on the belief system which their founder has left them as a legacy. They are now in the process of trying to formulate more clearly the essentials of their faith.

CHAPTER IV

RELIGIOUS RITUAL

SABBATH

The central act of religious worship among the Apostles of Johane Masowe is the weekly celebration of the Sabbath. The Sabbath runs from sundown on Friday to sundown on Saturday strictly speaking, but some Apostles in more recent times insist that it continues on to Sunday morning in accordance with Matthew 28:1. Apart from the intrinsic value of Sabbath worship to the Apostles themselves, it also acts as the principal means of making their presence known to others. Their harmonious singing of 'Hosanna' and other hymns can be heard for miles about, and this acts as a powerful attraction to outsiders. Apart from singing, the main emphasis during Sabbath prayer-services is on the Bible. Worship takes place in the open air, preferably close to a tree or some large rocks. Right from the start, *Baba* Johane had reacted against the use of church buildings, a policy which has given the Apostles greater freedom of movement without the burden of taxes for the construction and upkeep of such buildings. In the early days of the movement, the Apostles used to spend the complete Sabbath on a hillside, a custom which is still continued in the rural areas of Rhodesia. I have seen such gatherings in both Gandanzara and Dewedzo. In the sub-urban areas, however, the Apostles tend to gather in any spot which is convenient and they return to their homes at night.

During weekdays, Masowe women may wear light-coloured clothes although white is always recommended. During Sabbath, however, white dresses and white headdresses are obligatory. Dark colours, such as black and red, may never be worn. They believe that such colours connote blood, violence and death. Men used to wear some form of white covering during prayer-services, a custom which is still continued in some rural areas. When I attended a Sabbath at St. Mary's Township near Salisbury in 1974, most of the men wore white sheets (see fig. 7). In the sub-urban areas in general, however, this custom has dropped out, and the men are just expected to dress tidily. They are forbidden to wear ties as *Baba* Johane believed that ties connoted a form of pride which could lead to envy. The Apostles always remove their shoes during worship, a custom which is most probably based on the biblical precept in Exodus 3:5. Sundkler has suggested that the reason for the removal of shoes in many African religious movements

FIG. 7. Sabbath at St Mary's Township, Salisbury, Rhodesia, 1974.

is simply to enable the worshippers to dance to the rhythm of the drums more easily (1964, 196–7). This does not apply in the case of the Masowe Apostles, however, for they neither use drums nor allow dancing. In fact, they associate both of these activities with the evil pleasures of their past from which they have been called. Masowe men, unlike the men in similar religious movements (cf. Turner, 1967, 2:111; Jules-Rosette, 1973, 164, unpublished), do not use staffs. *Baba* Johane was the only one who used to hold a staff and he would only use it during the performance of baptisms. No musical instruments at all are used during Sabbath ritual and the clapping of hands is forbidden. The only object which the Apostles bring regularly to their worship services is a copy of the Bible. Irrespective of whether they can read it or not, it still holds a prestige value for them. Whenever a text is mentioned during a sermon, those with Bibles finger them anxiously. Of the three objects which Johane had in his possession when he first proclaimed his gospel message, viz., a Bible, a staff and a white garment, the Bible is the only one which has been retained by his followers. The white garment (for men) and the staff have largely been discarded.

Apart from Sabbath worship, the Apostles are expected to gather for prayer every morning as the sun rises and again as the sun sets. This custom was observed at the Masowe headquarters in Lusaka in 1974. It ought to be mentioned at this point that the description of Sabbath worship which follows is based on participant observation carried out at Marrapodi compound, Lusaka, between June and September 1974. This community of Apostles contains the main body of Sisters and, due to the split in the church, Sabbath services were carried on in their enclosure during these months. Hence, while the following description deals with the Masowe Sabbath, it must not be taken for granted that worship as carried out at Marrapodi is typical of that carried out in other Masowe communities. What we are dealing with is a privileged case. On the other hand, it would be rash to conclude that this basic structure is not observed elsewhere as well.

Framework of Masowe Sabbath observance

5:45 'Hosanna mukuru' (the great Hosanna) sung by all.
      Leader of prayer-service prays aloud.
      Collective personal prayer of praise, petition, and repentance.
      Hymn singing.
      The 'Our Father' recited in common.
      Prophets or preachers may speak at this point if they wish.
      Prayer-leader concludes the service.
9:00 Same as above but longer, as prophets or preachers usually speak.
14:30 'Hosanna mukuru' and other hymns sung by all.
      Leader of prayer-service announces names of those who will speak.
      Preaching and hymn singing intermingled.
      Prayer-leader concludes the service.
17:45 Same as for 5:45.
      Healing services normally take place at this time though they may take place at other times also.

Shortly before morning and evening prayer-services, an official caller can be heard moving around the village shouting out in the manner of a Mohammedan muezzin, '*Gadzirirai!*' (Prepare!). Then comes the cry, '*Fambai!*' (Hurry!), which is followed by the invitation, '*Pindai pamuteuro*' (enter the place of prayer). The place where the Apostles gather for prayer is technically referred to as *masowe* (wilderness), and the word can also be used to refer to Sabbath worship itself. As the white-clad women assemble in complete silence, they sit down on the ground waiting for the service to begin. The men, on the other hand, assemble either inside or around the *dare* shelter in which official business, as well as the exchange of information and news, is carried out (see fig. 8). In traditional Shona custom, the *dare* was the place where chiefs used to hold their court sessions, or where headmen or heads of families used to assemble for meetings. Among the

FIG. 8. Elders in *dare* shelter at Marrapodi, Lusaka, Zambia, 1974.

Maranke Apostles, the *dare* functions as a kind of gossip centre (See Jules-Rosette, 1973, 179).

When the service is ready to begin, all present remove their shoes and take up their respective positions for prayer. The ordained members (see pp. 102–8 below) take up their position in the front line with the unordained male adults and boys standing in line behind them. The Sisters stand in line behind them again and they in turn are followed by the married women and girls. All stand facing east, a custom which has both biblical and traditional roots (Ezekiel 8:16; Daneel, 1971, 80–90; see p. 97 below). When all are in position, the prayer-leader shouts '*Imbai!*' (Sing!), and all proceed to sing the great Hosanna. The only words used in this hymn are 'hosanna', 'gloria', and 'alleluia' which are repeated over and over again, either in part or in full. Singing is a very important mode of praying for the Apostles, and they believe that when they sing, they are joining with the angels in heaven who are continually worshipping God in this manner. The reference is apparently to Revelations 5:11, where it states that the angels were praising the lamb on the throne. Instead of using the word for lamb (*nyenye*), however, the Apostles always substitute the somewhat similar word for star (see p. 50 above). The Apostles frequently admonish one another for the poor quality of their singing and they insist that when they (and the Sisters in particular) sing, they are praying with the tongues of angels. One of the preachers spoke as follows:

> It was his plan, the plan of God himself, the plan of *Baba* Johane, which enabled us to get out of the fire and away from evil spirits. Today, we are

singing with his angels the glory which he gave us so that we might pray with them.[35]

Angelology, in fact, plays a prominent part in the Apostles' understanding of God's communication with man. The angels are looked upon as God's messengers, and it is for this reason that Johane Masowe himself has been described as the angel of God to Africa (see pp. 41 and 50 above). The angels are understood as a partial expression of the spirit of God (Sundkler, 1964, 249–50), and for this reason, they frequently communicate with the people through the prophets and 'teachers'. Angels have also held an important place in the belief of Maranke Apostles (*The New Witness of the Apostles,* n.d., 5, 13–14).

When the introductory singing to the morning and evening prayer-services has finished, the prayer-leader prays aloud to God to ask him to accept the prayers of all those who have come together to praise and worship him. The prayer-leader always begins by saying, 'Alleluia. In your name, Father, the son and the holy spirit', and ends by saying, 'Alleluia'. The use of the trinitarian formula, however, is not intended as an expression of belief in three persons in God, but rather as an invocation of Jehovah who expresses himself through his word and through his spirit (see pp. 47–9 above). When the prayer-leader has finished, all kneel down in personal prayer voiced aloud and remain either kneeling erect or crouched forward in such a way that their heads may even touch the ground. (This posture appears to be very similar to that of the Mohammedan posture for prayer, and another possible influence from Mohammedanism has also been noted in reference to the caller for prayer. I have not been able to establish any concrete proof of the direct influence of Moslem ritual and belief on the Masowe Apostles, but it is most probable that Mohammed's call as the prophet of the one God, Allah, did have a significant effect on Johane's awareness of his own call as the prophet of the one God, Jehovah, to the African races. The belief that the Arabian peoples also belonged to the line of Ham may well have suggested a certain similarity in the case of Johane's own vocation and that of Mohammed.)

The Apostles continue to pray in this posture for a period of about twenty minutes during which time the sun rises during the morning session and sets during the evening session. Originally, this period seems to have been devoted to a form of public confession. With the passage of time, however, the confession of crimes or offences committed seems to have dropped out, except for the admission of faults of

---

[35] Taped extract from sermon delivered at Marrapodi, Lusaka, on 13 July, 1974.

a very minor and rather general nature. At the same time, the technique of drowning the utterance of any particular individual in a sea of noise has continued. Everyone shouts at full volume during this period, and the children present are encouraged to do so as well, a practice which they seem to enjoy immensely. The main emphasis in the personal prayer of individuals nowadays, however, tends to be on the praise of God and the seeking of his benefits and blessings. For this reason, I have referred to these periods of prayer as periods of 'collective personal prayer of praise, petition, and repentance'. The Apostles normally shut their eyes during these sessions and they appear to become completely engrossed in their own prayer. (Due to the effect of the darkness and the loud din of voices, they seemed to pay very little attention to my presence. It was only with great difficulty that, later on, my Shona intrepreters were able to decipher the utterances of individual speakers with any degree of consistency.)

As the collective din from personal prayer begins to grow less and less, the women sense that it is time to begin singing. At first, only a few begin to sing, but gradually the volume of singing smothers the few remaining voices which have continued to pray. All are quickly united in song. When the singing has ceased, the prayer-leader begins the 'Our Father' to which all join in. After this, there is a pause during which any prophets or preachers who may have arranged to speak stand up and address the crowd. They tend to speak more at length at the 9:00 prayer-services than during those in the early morning or in the evening. If there are speakers, all present sit down on the ground to listen. When the speakers have finished, the prayer-leader stands up and concludes the prayer-service encouraging all to keep the Sabbath holy and to return to the remaining prayer-services. The morning and evening prayer-services last for about forty-five minutes each, whereas the 9:00 prayer-service may continue for well over an hour.

The 14:30 prayer-service usually continues for the whole afternoon and runs automatically into the period for evening prayer. This means that the session continues for over four hours without a break. The Apostles, however, feel free to come and go as they please during this session and the atmosphere is very relaxed. The monotony is broken by the continual interspersal of preaching and singing, although much depends on the quality of the speakers. The choice, number, and order of speakers is decided on beforehand, and no other person may speak. The one exception to this rule concerns the 'teacher' to whom I shall refer shortly (see pp. 84–8 below). Speakers of lesser importance speak first and the more important ones, such as evangelists or visiting speakers, speak last. Sometimes, preaching is restricted to prophets alone; at other times, to preachers alone. Women may not speak, except in the case of a female prophet or 'teacher'.

The 14:30 prayer-service begins with the singing of the great Hosanna and other hymns. If any of the main speakers have been delayed, the singing continues. After the singing, the prayer-leader greets those present with the words, 'Peace be to you, Apostles', to which all reply, 'Amen'. The greeting, however, may be varied by using phrases like, 'Happiness be to you, Apostles', or 'Peace be to you, people of God'. The word 'peace' may just be repeated in some cases, viz., 'Peace, peace', and the response may change from 'Amen' to 'Alleluia'. The prayer-leader then announces the names of those who will be speaking and introduces any visitors who may be present. He reminds people that they have come to listen to the word of God and encourages all to pay attention and to listen carefully to what will be said. He then beckons to the first speaker to come forward and, while he is taking up his place, the Apostles begin to sing.

Speakers are usually accompanied by Bible readers who stand beside them holding their Bibles open. Whenever a speaker wants to comment on a passage or verse from the Bible, he will first ask the reader to read aloud the relevant parts. Speakers are also frequently accompanied by translators who stand beside them as well. This is becoming a more common practice nowadays among the Apostles on account of the fact that so many non-Shona may be present among the congregation. Shona, however, still tends to be the principal language of the Apostles, and converts are encouraged to become familiar with it. Sundkler mentions that, when the Apostles were in Port Elizabeth, Shona was regarded as the sacred language through which the Apostles had become the chosen people (1964, 249–50). I could find little evidence for this belief today, however.

Preachers. The standard of preaching among the Apostles varies enormously from preacher to preacher. Some preachers tend to repeat almost verbatim and without commentary the words of a verse from the Bible which has just been read out. Others say the same thing in only slightly different words. These preachers then rapidly greet the congregation and call for another reading from the Bible. It sometimes happens that what the preacher says has little or nothing to do with the verse of the Bible which has just been read. In such cases, it would seem that the preacher has already decided on what he wants to say and only calls for Bible readings as a matter of form. While this form of preaching, however, may give the impression of being eminently boring, it is extraordinary how some preachers can hold the attention of the congregation by the rhythmical effect of the continual and rapid interplay of Bible verse reading, greeting, congregational response, brief comment or repetition of verse, greeting, congregational response, another Bible reading, and so on, as the cycle continues.

On the other hand, some preachers tend to give long discourses on Bible passages as a form of religious instruction. In such cases, the message of the Bible is applied in a fundamentalist fashion to the Apostles themselves. It is not unusual for such preachers to continue for half an hour to an hour with few readings from the Bible. On account of their personal religious conviction and oratorical skills, they are capable of commanding the attention of their audience. At the same time, their preaching is regularly interspersed with singing.

Singing is the most effective way in which the main body of Apostles are enabled to participate in the Sabbath ritual. They can sing at almost any time they wish, and this gives them some control over the course of the prayer-service. One person, usually a woman, starts a hymn and others then join in. The introduction of a hymn acts as a very effective mechanism for preventing boredom, especially in the case of a monotonous or uninteresting speaker. The very frequent introduction of a hymn during a sermon can also act as a form of admonition to the speaker expressing the congregation's restlessness.

The preacher, for his part, may use the techniques of greeting or singing for his own purposes. If he feels that he is losing the attention of his audience, he may introduce frequent greetings in order to keep them attentive. He may also use a greeting as a means of emphasising a point which he has just made. If a preacher wants a short pause in which to rest or to think about what he is going to say next, he may introduce a hymn himself. Once a hymn has been begun by any one person, it normally triggers an automatic response from the whole congregation. In the case of important speakers, however, they may block the hymn from the start by a firm gesture if they feel that time is running out or that they have something important to say.

Another effective means of drawing the congregation more fully into the spirit of Sabbath worship is the technique of carrying on a dialogue with those present. An example of the use of such a technique was demonstrated during the 9:00 prayer-service on 13 July, 1974 at Marrapodi, Lusaka. The preacher was exhorting the congregation to have the right spirit when making financial contributions:

Preacher: Peace be to you, Apostles.
Congregation: Amen.
Preacher: I think we said the same thing yesterday. We want to ask ourselves what kind of a thing a gift is. Mothers, what is meant by a gift?
Congregation: It was established by God.

Preacher: What prompted God to say that people should give him gifts? Fathers, what made God say that people should give him gifts?

Congregation: In order to show their love for him.

Preacher: Do we really know that it was God who said that people should give gifts, that it was he who laid down the law that those who pray should give gifts? Who was told by God that people should offer him gifts?

Congregation: It was Moses.

Preacher: Yes, Moses. But why was Moses told that people should give gifts to God? Can God eat food or use money? Why, then, did he ask for gifts?

Congregation: It was in order to set apart those who believe in him.

Preacher: Yes, those who believe in God. Do we believe that it was God himself who established it, or was it people, priests or others, who said that it was from God?

Congregation: It was God himself who said it.

Preacher: What we are saying now is that we do not want anyone making an offering because he is being forced to do so. A person should give with a good heart knowing that this is something which was established by God himself.

The question and answer form of the above dialogue illustrates the manner in which a form of religious instruction can be given during a Sabbath prayer-service. The questions asked are really rhetorical in nature for they suggest the answers which are automatically elicited from the congregation. Nevertheless, a climate of personal contact is established between the preacher and the congregation which proves to be most effective.

Type I prophets. All ordained members among the Apostles may preach, viz., evangelists, preachers, prophets, and councillors (see pp. 102–8 below). The prophets tend to appropriate to themselves the prophetic books of the Bible (as well as the Book of Enoch), and the Books of Daniel and Revelations are very popular. The prophets are expected to be very familiar with all the prophetic utterances of the Bible and to be able to apply them appropriately to the Apostles themselves. The Bible, however, is not the only means by which the voice of God speaks to the prophets; indeed, it is primarily through dreams and visions that the prophets establish contact with God. These are the traditionally accepted modes of communication between human beings and the spirit world and, as such, they require little justification when used by the prophets as channels of their knowledge. The language of the prophets is frequently clothed in symbolic imagery which tends to reflect the form of expression of the biblical prophets. The following illustration is taken from a Sabbath prayer-service held on 29 June, 1974 at Marrapodi, Lusaka, at 5:45:

... When I was praying here, I saw a river which ran in front of a mountain. As I kept looking, I saw a person on top of it and there were sheep
grazing at the bottom. I kept on looking at the sheep to see where they
were going. They were looking in the direction of the mountain and were
trying to cross the river to get to it. I saw another person going round the
mountain trying to rescue the person who was on top, and a voice said,
'Behold, the one you see going round the mountain is the evangelist, and
the one on top of the mountain is the shepherd'. As I kept on looking at
the person on top, I saw that he was covered in many colours from head to
feet. The colours, however, were not those of clothes but of wounds.

As I kept on looking, the person on top of the mountain kept on bid-
ding his sheep to come to him, and the sheep flocked into the river. The
goats were moving about trying to find a way to cross over the river, but
they failed to find the path used by the sheep. I asked what was happening
and it was said, 'They see fire where the sheep are crossing so they cannot
pass'.

I kept on looking at the man on top of the mountain and he was very
powerful. It was said, 'I want you to make the sheep go to the mountain to
where that man is'. Then, I asked about his wounds as to what kind they
were. It was said, 'They are real wounds. They will affect those who go
astray. He is the king of wounds'.

Then, I saw the goats sinking in the river. As I kept on looking, the
mountain began to recede in size as all the sheep with no wounds got to it.
Then, I saw the sheep coming here. As I kept on looking, I was told that
the wounds will be coming here. That is the end.

This vision bears the clear imprint of Enoch 89:28–40 and Ezekiel 34.
On the other hand, it has been re-created in such a way as to apply to
the very concrete circumstances of the time. The message, in this case,
was unmistakable. The division among the Apostles had been at its
height, and great numbers had been joining the rebel group. The vision described by the prohet painted the picture of Johane Masowe on
top of the mountain of the Lord covered in wounds which he had
received from the rebel group. The evangelist of the loyalist followers
of Johane (i.e., the sheep) was leading them safely across the river,
whereas the rebel group (i.e., the goats) was unable to cross.

During Sabbath services, prophets make a variety of guttural
sounds at regular intervals, particularly on days when they are
expected to speak. Whenever they do stand up to speak, they always
begin by producing these sounds. Daneel has written of traditional
Shona religion that 'it is essential that the spirit indicates its presence
through grunts, snorts, hissing sounds, monosyllabic cries, writhing of
the body or high-pitched monologues ...' (1971, 149). Among the
Masowe prophets, such sounds follow recognised patterns, one of the
most noticeable being like that of the braying of a donkey. The pur-

pose of making these sounds is to emphasise their prophetic role and to demonstrate that the spirit of God is taking hold of them. They sway their heads to and fro, closing their eyes and tightening the muscles of their necks and faces in such a way as if to suggest that they are attempting to resist some force which is proceeding to take possession of them. Once they have completed this demonstration, however, they can become perfectly normal and relaxed as they proceed to make known their revelations or exhort the congregation. There is, in fact, a basis in traditional forms of spirit possession for this restrained mode of behaviour. I have not observed among these prophets any of the exaggerated or highly emotional forms of ecstatic frenzy which are more often said to be characteristic of the more traditional Shona forms of spirit possession. The prophets always remain sitting down until their time comes to speak. Then, they continue to remain standing in one spot without making any dance-like movements or wild gesticulations with their hands.

The imagery used by the prophets is not always biblically inspired and it may deal with such commonplace objects as a rock in the ground, mason wasps or a football match. When relating their dreams and visions, they use biblical prophetic catch-phrases, such as, 'as I kept on looking'. The relationship between God and the prophets is considered to be a very familiar one so that the prophets wield great power and influence among the Apostles. Like Enoch, they walk with God (Gen. 5:22, 24); hence, they are expected to pray more frequently and more intensely than other Apostles. The following revelation was expressed by a prophet at Marrapodi, Lusaka, during the time that the split among the Apostles was causing much concern, and it demonstrates the familiar, almost casual, relationship between Jehovah and the prophet:

> I dreamt that the evil spirit had got into this village. . . . While I was kneeling here, tears came out as I was talking with Jehovah. I asked what had happened. I said, 'Is it true?' Then God, speaking into my ears, said, 'What are you asking?' I answered, 'I'm asking about these things which you have shown me'. Then he answered . . . 'Didn't I tell you that the evil spirit hasn't finished yet!' . . . As I continued speaking with God, he said . . . 'Don't be frightened. It won't happen that this church will be destroyed by any man. I, Jehovah, will stop that evil spirit'. . . . Then I said, 'I understand, Lord'. God then said, 'Tell my people who are here that the holy spirit is here'.

The manner in which the prophet relates to God in the extract above reveals an attitude towards a personal, loving and concerned God which is a major breakthrough from the traditional distant and awesome God of the Shona. The prophets are looked upon as the light of the Apostles, and they are expected—as in the dream above—to reassure the people of God's help in time of trial.

Type II prophets ('teachers'). There is a second type of prophet among the Apostles through whom the spirit of God speaks to the people in a direct manner. This type of prophet is commonly referred to as a *svikiro* or spirit medium (see pp. 47, 102), or as a 'teacher' (*mudzidzisi*). The spirit of God may speak through a 'teacher' at any time and, when this happens, all must listen. The 'teachers' claim to be aware of what they are saying at all times and—contrary to traditional Shona spirit mediums (Gelfand, 1973, 134)—they can remember clearly afterwards all that they have said. When a 'teacher' speaks in a formal oracular capacity (i.e., teaches with the spirit), it is God himself who is believed to be speaking (Cf. Daneel, 1971, 100). 'Teachers' will frequently preface their remarks with the phrase, 'God is saying . . .' in order to emphasise their role as intermediaries and, in like manner, they may say, '*Baba* Johane is saying . . .'. They are also gifted with the spirit of tongues, a characteristic which distinguishes them from those who have the spirit of prophecy. The same person, however, may have both gifts. As a 'teacher' may speak in a tongue which cannot be understood by those present, an interpreter is usually called for when a 'teacher' is speaking. In traditional Shona religion, each spirit medium had an acolyte (*nechombo*) who performed this function. As Gelfand has said: 'The people can hear what the *mhondoro* says through his medium, but if there is any difficulty in interpretation, it is the duty of the *nechombo* to explain the meaning to the delegates' (Gelfand, 1962, 23). Among the Masowe Apostles, women can become both prophets and 'teachers,' and one of the most prominent 'teachers' at present is also one of the Sisters. This 'teacher' taught with the spirit one day during a Sabbath prayer-service at which I was present.

The day was a particularly important one because a Government official had come to address the congregation. In his address, he sided with the elders against the younger ones who had broken away and he referred to the Apostles as a 'church of the elders'. When he had finished speaking, the 'teacher', who had been sitting in the back with the other Sisters, suddenly stood up and indicated that the spirit of God wanted to say something. Once she had stood up, all those who had been facing east turned around to face her, so that now everybody present was looking at her. This demonstrated the realisation on the part of all that the spirit of God was now present in a special way and was working through his 'teacher'. The 'teacher' made unintelligible sounds for about half a minute and then she called for the chief evangelist present. He answered her and, from then on, he began to act as an interpreter in what she said. At first he repeated almost verbatim almost every sentence she uttered prefacing his remarks by the phrase, 'It is said . . .'. She once used the phrase, 'Baba Johane is saying . . .'. At times the evangelist altered slightly the words she had used in order to make the meaning more clear. Finally the 'teacher' had become so absorbed in what she was saying that she didn't wait for the evangelist to explain what she had said but just continued to speak at a very rapid pace. The evangelist barely managed to inject a few explanatory remarks every now and then. During her discourse, the 'teacher' paused a number of times either to utter strange sounds, to sing alone, to lead a hymn in which she was followed by the congregation, or to address rhetorical questions either to the congregation or to the evangelist himself. Her teaching ended with an out-pouring of strange sounds once again. What follows, then, is an extract from the instruction given by 'teacher' Esima at Marrapodi, Lusaka, on 6 July, 1974. Evangelist Cyprian Nedewedzo acted as interpreter. The 'teacher' will be referred to as 'she' and the evangelist as 'he'—*only* when the words of the evangelist differ from those of the 'teacher' will they be quoted:

She: Evangelist Luke, I have very little to say.
She: [Makes prophetic sounds] I say that you [pl.] are blessed.
She: You saw the power of *Baba* Johane.
He: Because you saw the power of *Baba* Johane.
She: You know that *Baba* Johane is god who descended from heaven.
She: *Baba* Johane is saying, 'I want to speak with him' [i.e., the Government official].
She: [Makes prophetic sounds] *Baba* Johane descended from heaven in the year 1932.
She: He was born as a child in the country of Rhodesia.
She: The spirit of God (*mudzimu waMwari*) descended from heaven, the word of God (*izwi raMwari*).
He: The word of God descended on him.
She: It came and rested on him.
He: It came and rested on his head.
She: It came and called from the top of the mountain to the people of Africa, the sons of this house of Ham (*imba yaHam*).
She: It called from the top of the mountain saying, 'Fear God and praise him, for the time of his rule is at hand' [see Rev. 14:7].
She: He came and proclaimed, 'I have come to the descendants of the children of Ham'.
She: 'I have not come to the white people. The rule of the white people has come to an end.'
He: It is said, 'He came proclaiming that the rule of the white people had

come to an end. He said that Africa now wants to rule itself'.

She: He proclaimed from the top of the mountain

She: Saying

She: [Begins to sing and all join in]

She: He came saying, 'I have come to save the children of the house of Ham because, on that day in the time of Noah, God cursed the house of Ham and blessed Shem and Jepheth'.

She: The time for their captivity has expired.

She: It is *Baba* Johane who has assembled this congregation.

He: It is *Baba* Johane who has assembled all the people including this congregation.

She: That is what Johane saw on the island of Patmos.

He: That is the new vision which Johane had on the island of Patmos.

She: It is said, 'I saw some people garbed in white following the star [*sic*—see p. 50 above] wherever it went' [see Rev. 14:4].

She: This is the congregation assembled by *Baba* Johane.

He: This is the congregation assembled here which is wearing white clothes.

She: It is called 'the liberation of Africa from bondage'.

She: [Makes prophetic sounds] There is a group which has been specially chosen in this congregation [i.e., the Sisters, see pp. 62–9 above].

She: This is the group which has been placed in the middle of this village.

She: You must look after this group in a royal manner.

She: If you destroy it or let it be destroyed

She: The world will go back into the darkness where it was before

She: This group is called 'the salvation of Africa' (*ruponiso rweAfrica*).

She: It is called 'the mother of Africa'

She: Who prays for Africa so that it might be saved.

She: They [*sic*] were given by Baba Johane so that they might be able to save [people] in this life and in the life of the spirit.

She: Let this man here [i.e., Government official] listen properly.

He: It is said, 'Let this man of God here listen properly'.

She: You chased away into the darkness the white people who were ruling here.

She: If you do not handle properly that which has been placed in the centre of Africa [i.e., the Sisters], they [i.e., the white people] might come again like clouds and darken Africa.

He: If you do not handle this light properly, they [i.e., the white people] will come again and cover Africa just like the clouds, and you will return once more into bondage.

She: Do you understand?

He: Yes, it is being understood.

She: Look after it [i.e., the Sisters]. It is called 'the salvation of Africa'.

She: It is our shade to protect us from the sun.

She: Do they understand?

He: Yes, they understand.

She: *Baba* Johane sang thus in Rhodesia:

She: [Sings] 'Let *Baba* Elijah conquer the darkness in Africa,

as he once did in Jerusalem;
Let Jehovah conquer the darkness in Africa,
as he once did in Jerusalem.'
Evangelist Luke, I want you to ask a small question for me. When the government in this country came into power, was there much bloodshed as there has been in other countries?

He: They say, 'No'.

She: If that is so, do they know the reason why?

He: It is because of the spirit of God.

She: It is true. It is because of the word of God which had already been in this land which helped you. You must look after it so that it may maintain your Government for a long time. If there is an enemy who wants to destroy the Government, you must know who that enemy is. You must know where the truth of God is so that, in this way, you may be able to continue to rule for a long time. These are the words which I wanted to say to this man here [i.e. the Government official—this man had been a friend of the Apostles since their arrival in Zambia and he was not present in an official capacity at this time].

He: These are the words that I wanted to tell him so I called him back.

She: Did he hear that?

He: Yes. He says, 'Thank you'.

She: [Begins to sing 'Hosanna' and all join in].

She: Let the rulers of the earth listen.

She: You were given power to rule the world.

She: Do not co-operate with those who want to destroy the house of Jehovah [i.e., the rebel group of Apostles].

He: Do not co-operate with those who want to destroy the kingdom of God, the house of God.

She: If there are some who want to destroy the house of Jehovah, let them do it without your support. They should not rely on you.

She: They must not be allowed to depend on you. They must not be allowed to depend on you.

She: They will bring fire into your kingdom.

She: Because Jehovah's eye is as red as the flames of fire.

She: This is what we are telling this man.

He: This is what we are telling the servant of the Governor.

She: There are Government officials who are superior to him.

She: [Addressing the official] You are to be a witness to what we are saying.

She: So that your Government may not lose favour with God.

She: This group is called 'holy' (kuyera).

She: It is called 'holy'.

She: It is called 'righteous' (kururama).

She: It is called 'the love of Jehovah himself' (rudo rwaJehovah pachake iye).

She: I have finished.

He: Alleluia.

She: [Begins to sing alone in tongues: 'Rigindi marigarigarindi arigindi marigarindi. . .']

He: Mr G. [i.e., the Government official] wants to say something.

She: You may speak.

[The Government official—who is not a Shona—speaks in English and thanks the 'teacher' for what she has said. He emphasises that the holy spirit is with the church of the elders which is the true church. Then, he leaves and the 'teacher' begins to speak again.]

She: [Continues to sing alone in tongues as above]

She: Evangelist, do not be surprised.

She: Now is our time to give a chance to the rulers to know the house of Jehovah.

She: It is our time to teach them.

She: This time, we are still climbing. We will get to the top pf the mountain. We are still pointing towards the mountain.

She: [Makes prophetic sounds]

She: We are going to speak to them in a language that they will understand.

She: Do you [pl.] understand?

Congregation: Yes.

She: We are going to speak about this house to kings. We are climbing up the mountain with it. It has to be known by the whole world. Do you understand, men and women?

Congregation: Yes.

She: The word of God must spread out until the end. [Makes prophetic sounds] We do not believe that *Baba* Johane is dead, but we know that he is alive. If someone dies today, will it strengthen the kingdom? We only know that it signifies the spreading of the word of God to all races. We are going to Ethiopia and we will pass through Ethiopia on our way to Egypt and to Jerusalem. The spirit of God is sending us to all these places. Do you understand?

Congregation: Yes.

She: [Makes prophetic sounds].

Preachers and prophets, then, place a different emphasis on the source of their knowledge during Sabbath prayer-services. Whereas the prophets refer to the word of God as contained in the Bible (as do the preachers), they also attribute their knowledge to the direct working of the spirit of God within them. No contradiction, however, is seen in the two channels of knowledge, for the source of both is the same. It is Jehovah himself who is communicating with his people through the medium of his word in the Bible and through the action of his spirit in the prophets.

At the end of the Sabbath prayer-service, when all the speakers have finished, the prayer-leader sums up what each of the speakers has said. He encourages the Apostles to be faithful to the teaching which they have received and concludes the meeting. The people then go back to their homes, the women leaving first and then the men.

Every Apostle is expected to make a contribution towards the welfare of his own congregation for the needs of the aged and the sick and for the upkeep of those who continue to move about spreading the word of God in other places. Such collections are usually made after each prayer-service during the Sabbath, and certain individuals are appointed to write down the names and amounts of those who have contributed. Sermons are constantly focused on the importance of these contributions for the growth and spread of the work which had been entrusted by God to Johane and his followers.

HEALING

Rituals of healing play a major part in many African religious movements and, in some of them, regular healing centres have been established (Sundkler, 1964, 220–37; Becken, 1972, 213–22; Turner, 1967, 2:141–58). This is not so, however, in the case of the Masowe Apostles. They do, indeed, have prayer-healing services, but they are rather simple affairs. This is not to suggest that the Apostles do not consider the need for healing to be important; they do. On the other hand, psychosomatic healing is seen as part of the much wider need for salvific healing which finds its principal source in the word of God. Like the Church of the Lord, Aladura (Cf. Turner, 1967, 2:83–4, 328–30), the Masowe Apostles are today primarily a biblically oriented religious movement. This, however, does not seem to have been the case in the early days of the movement when the emphasis on spirit-healing was much more exaggerated than it is today. In those days, the awareness of possession by evil spirits was much stronger than it is today, and the role of the prophets was seen very much in terms of their ability to diagnose the source of evil and reveal hidden objects of witchcraft. Healing by the spirit of God could only take place when the guilty persons confessed to their evil ways and handed up their witchcraft preparations. An example of such an occurrence can be found in a police file for June 1934 which is kept at the National Archives of Rhodesia. The description runs as follows:

> The inhabitants of one or more kraals are gathered together in an open space nearby and placed in single line to form a circle. The 'Prophets' and 'Disciples' take up positions in the centre of the circle and commence to pray and chant, invoking the Holy Spirit to enter into their bodies. The 'Prophet' or 'Prophets', if more than one is present, work themselves into a state of religious fervour and finally lose control of themselves. In this state, they commence to go round the congregation and point out persons who are witches who possess medicines or charms with which to harm others. In some cases, definite accusations have been made. Those pointed

out by the 'Prophets' are called upon to confess their sins and produce all medicines and charms in their possession. In one instance, it is alleged that three 'Prophets' accused a woman of causing the death of her husband, the kraal headman, by means of witchcraft (File 26).

This example does not, in fact, refer directly to the followers of Johane Masowe, but to those who had been in the company of one Takundwa. This Takundwa, however, was known to have been a close associate of Johane and it had been reported in an earlier document (File 10) that 'vestments and crucifixes belonging to Shoniwa' had been found in his possession. It is reasonable, therefore, to assume that the behaviour of Takundwa's followers would have borne a close resemblance to that of the followers of Johane. The difference between the 'Prophets' and the 'Disciples' mentioned above is that the former 'claimed to have divine power to heal the sick through the Holy Spirit' whereas the latter, who were also called 'Apostles,' 'were supporters of the "Prophets" and did not possess their divine power of healing' (File 26). This emphasis on healing by the power of the holy spirit had been due, apparently, to the influence of Apostolic Faith Mission preachers (Files 21, 23, 26) and Johane had clearly begun to substitute the healing power of the holy spirit through prayer for the traditional healing powers of the diviner-herbalist.[36] It is significant that the one danger which AFM preachers and the prophets of Johane Masowe had to guard against in conducting such practices was that of contravening the Witchcraft Suppression Ordinance of 1899.

Healing services among the Apostles of Johane Masowe today are technically referred to as *'kuita* "ground," ' which means, 'to form a circle'. The use of the English word 'ground' may be an erroneous use of the word 'round' for 'circle'. It would appear that, in the early days, the girls would move about in a circle singing while the holy spirit was being invoked to take possession of certain individuals. In the case of healing services today, the women do form a circle but they do not move about as they sing. The Sisters only take part in this if there are no other women present. The hymns they sing are 'Come, holy spirit' and 'All-powerful Jehovah, you have created all things, alleluia, gloria, hosanna, gloria'. While they are singing, those to be healed enter into the circle and kneel down. Pregnant mothers enter first and then the others. A few may move in at the same time. Any of the ordained Apostles may perform the laying on of hands for healing, and I have

---

[36] On 5th December, 1934, the Assistant Native Commissioner, Goromonzi, had written to the Chief Native Commissioner, Salisbury, as follows: '. . . I found that John's work consisted of baptising anybody not yet baptised and that his sole teaching was that sickness could be cured by faith and prayer, and that prayer could be as effectively performed in the hut or veldt as could be in any Church.' (See File 30).

been told that it is very important for the healer to sympathise with the sick person in order that the cure may be fully effective.[37] As the healers place their hands on the heads of the sick people, they pray that the holy spirit may send down his healing power through them. The Masowe Apostles do not use holy water or healing sticks (Cf. Murphree, 1969, 102) and, contrary to the practice of the Maranke Apostles, (Cf. Jules-Rosette, 1973, 29), they do not allow women to become healers.

Healing services are only attended by small numbers and they usually take place after the evening Sabbath service has ended. The Apostles acknowledge the strong hold which belief in traditional spirits still has over many of their people and they counteract it with the stronger power of the holy spirit (see p. 125 below). They believe that sin and evil are closely linked together and that the former is the root cause of the latter. All forms of sickness are seen to be connected with the powers of evil with the result that only the power of the holy spirit can bring about healing. Such healing, however, requires confident recourse through prayer to the holy spirit, and the use of any physical medicines is looked upon as a failure to trust wholeheartedly in the power of God. The Apostles do allow the use of medicines, however, in certain situations. When they arrived in Plumtree, Rhodesia, in 1962 after their deportation from South Africa, they reluctantly allowed themselves to be vaccinated. A similar situation arose during a smallpox epidemic in Zambia in 1964 (Dobney, 1964, 9), Furthermore, they go to hospitals in the case of serious cuts or accidents. At the same time, while recognising the effectiveness of certain modern forms of medicine, they preserve the integrity of their belief by insisting that the use of such medicines incurs defilement. Hence, prayer over the person who intends to receive medicine is necessary both before and after treatment. Such a person may not participate in Sabbath worship until a purification ceremony has been performed.

In sum, then, healing services do play a part in the struggle of the Apostles against the powers of evil. These services, however, do not receive major emphasis and must be seen in the context of the fuller belief of the Apostles, viz., that the most radical form of healing is brought about by listening to, and observing, the word of God. Hence, the major emphasis is upon the Bible during Sabbath worship.

BAPTISM

The ritual of baptism is one which had always been an essential part of the mission which had been entrusted to Johane Masowe. It is for this

[37] Biblical texts used concerning healing are: Mk. 16:18; James 5:15; Ex. 15:26; Acts 6:4.

very purpose that he had been given a new identity as John the Baptist for African races (see p. 57 above). During his lifetime, he had insisted that every one of his followers would have to undergo the ritual of baptism. This was true even for those who had been baptised already in other churches. During a Sabbath service in 1974, an evangelist expressed it as follows:

> Some of you may have been baptised in the synagogues [i.e., the established churches]. You may wonder, then, why he [i.e., *Baba* Johane] had to baptise you again. The reason is that you did not have the holy spirit. You were like the disciples of John, the son of Zachary, who did not have the holy spirit.

Apparently, the Apostles had come to a clearer understanding of the difference between baptism of repentance and baptism of the holy spirit. The latter could only result from the spirit of Jesus, and Johane Masowe was the one who had brought this spirit to Africans. Johane himself was, in fact, the only person who could baptise during his lifetime, for he believed that he was the only one who had been entrusted with that power by God. After his death, however, a major problem arose among his followers. If, on the one hand, baptism was essential for the salvation of Africans, then it could not be discarded. On the other hand, since Johane himself was the only one who had the authority to baptise, how could the practice be continued after his death? The dilemma could not be avoided. Even during the lifetime of Johane, his adamant refusal to allow others to perform baptisms had begun to cause some anxiety. The number of Masowe followers had begun to increase so rapidly that it had become no longer possible for one person to baptise them all. Reference has already been made to the fact that in 1959 Johane had made a tour around congregations in Southern Rhodesia, Northern Rhodesia and Nyasaland baptising adults and children, a tour which had taken two and a half years. From 1964 onwards, however, when he had become ill, no baptisms had been performed. Johane believed that he would get well again and that he would then be able to continue with his work of baptising. In fact, he had been particularly anxious that the Kikuyu Apostles in Kenya might not find out about his presence in Nairobi in 1973 until he would be well enough to baptise them.[38] By this time, the Apostles had

---

[38] The baptismal photograph on page 182 of the *Kenya Churches Handbook* has been erroneously attributed to the Masowe Apostles (Gospel of God) as Johane Masowe never carried out baptisms in Kenya, nor is he the baptiser in the photograph—see David B. Barrett, George K. Mambo, Janice McLaughlin and Malcolm J. McVeigh, eds., *Kenya Churches Handbook: The Development of Kenyan Christianity 1498–1973* (Evangel Publishing House, P.O. Box 969, Kisumu, Kenya. n.d.).

also begun to expand into Zaire and they had become very concerned over the time when all of these new adherents might be baptised. Johane had repeatedly insisted, however, that he could not share with, or delegate to, anyone else the authority to baptise with which he alone had been invested by God.

In the Synod at Gandanzara in 1974, the loyalist Apostles faced up to the dilemma concerning the continuation of the ritual of baptism. The decision they came to was that the supreme council of seventy members would have the authority to appoint baptisers. This decision, however, was later on questioned once again by some members on the basis that the Head Sister living at Nairobi had not been present at the Synod. She had failed to obtain the required travel documents in time. *Mai* Meggi Matanhire (see fig. 6 on p. 66 above) had always been very close to Johane and on a question so important as that of baptism, her understanding of the mind of Johane was considered to be of major importance. It would appear that she had insisted that Johane had never intended that anyone else should continue his uniquely special work of baptising. So the dilemma concerning baptism still remains.

The manner in which baptisms (or Jordans) were performed by Johane Masowe was described to me as follows: All those to be bap-

FIG. 9. Apostles beside fallen altar on Mount Nyahawa, Wedza, Rhodesia.

tised would be gathered together at a river. (In the case of there not being a river sufficiently close by, baptisms could be performed by sprinkling from a basin of water). Johane Masowe would stand in the middle of the river dressed in a white garment. Samson Mativera (see p. 51 above), his personal attendant, would stand on one side holding a small cross and a bowl of blood taken from a lamb or a pigeon. The number one evangelist, who was then Saizi Sithole (see p. 53 above), would stand at his other side. Some girls (now Sisters) would begin to sing so that the water might be purified and so that evil spirits might be driven from the water and from those to be baptised. The candidates for baptism would walk between two lines of prophets (the gateway of the prophets), passing by the major prophet, Samuel Chinyanga (see fig. 11, p. 115 below), last of all. An evangelist would then escort the candidates to *Baba* Johane, who would immerse them completely in the water three times baptising them in the name of the Father, the son and the holy spirit. Then, he would dip his finger in the bowl of blood and mark the sign of the cross on the forehead of each one. In the case of babies to be baptised, water would be poured over their foreheads.

The Murphree essay mentions that the body of the animal whose blood was used during baptisms was burnt on a pile of wood: 'The smoke is expected to go up to heaven to show the people that the work is well done and has been accepted by God.'[39] This practice was apparently based on an Old Testament injunction and would appear to have been rather short-lived. When I was escorted by Masowe followers to the Wedza Tribal Trust Land in Rhodesia, they brought me up on top of a solid mountain of rock called Nyahawa to show me the fallen remains of the altar which their founder had built there (see fig. 9). Onias Bvuma explained the significance of this altar to me later on:

> *Baba* Johane built this altar intending to make burnt offerings of sheep on it. When he had finished building it, however, he said to me: 'I built this altar intending it to be a place where burnt offerings could be made, but now I have changed my mind. Now I want it to be a place where any of you people from Dewedzo may come if you have any serious illness, or if there is a drought in the country. The spirit will tell you to go to the mountain of Nyahawa and to bring some girls with you to sing while you pray. The illness and the drought will then cease. It is these girls who will move about with me and sing at Jordans.

The reference to the burning of a sheep on an altar built on a mountain is very reminiscent of Abraham's sacrifice as described in Genesis

[39] Marshall W. Murphree, 'The History, Doctrines and Organisation of the Johane Masowe Vapostori', p. 32. This forty-page essay, which Professor Murphree has kindly allowed me to use, is the result of data collected by two research assistants at Seki and Gandanzara respectively between 22 December, 1966 and 26 January, 1967.

22. When Johane used the blood of a young sheep during baptisms and then consumed its body in fire, he may well have been mingling Genesis 22 with Revelations 7:4 and 1 John 5:6–8. The signing of the cross with blood, however, has no connection in the minds of the Apostles with suffering or with the death of Jesus. Cyprian Nedewedzo told me that the cross signifies the four corners of the earth to which the gospel must be preached.

MARRIAGE

Polygamous marriages are the accepted custom among the Apostles, and most men try to have as many wives as possible. Fidelity within the polygamous marriage system, however, is rigidly insisted upon and sexual relationships outside of marriage can lead to suspension or even expulsion. The Apostles are not allowed to marry non-believers, and parents are not allowed to receive '*lobola*' (bride-price) when giving their daughters in marriage. Premarital relations are strictly forbidden, and permission must be obtained from the parents of both parties as well as from the proper religious authorities before a marriage can take place.

Jules-Rosette (1973, 233) has mentioned that the Maranke Apostles do not hold an elaborate marriage ceremony of either the traditional or the Western type. The same is true of the Masowe Apostles for the wedding ceremony is a very simple affair. When the necessary permissions have been obtained, a day is chosen for the wedding during the week, for it is forbidden to hold a marriage ceremony on the Sabbath. The whole congregation assembles, and the bride dresses in a long white dress. An evangelist must be present to perform the ceremony and prophets must be present to scrutinise the couple.

As the ceremony begins, the whole congregation is singing. When the singing stops, the evangelist beckons to the couple to come forward. The prophets who are present point out any obstacles which may prevent the couple from getting married. If such obstacles do not exist, then the prophets reveal any difficulties which they foresee may endanger the marriage and warn the couple of possible pitfalls. After this, a circle is formed as in healing ceremonies and the evangelist places his hands on the heads of the couple and prays for them. The prophets and the rest of the congregation are asked to pray for them also. The evangelist then joins the hands of the couple together and declares them husband and wife. Singing continues at intervals during the ceremony and, when it is finished, the new wife goes to her husband's house on the same day. No wedding rings are passed between the couple and no beast is killed for a celebration. If the husband happens to have other wives, he will normally have discussed taking a new wife with them beforehand thereby obtaining their approval.

ORDINATION

The Masowe Apostles believe that all of those who are ordained have been chosen by the holy spirit of Jehovah, and that it is through them as his 'workers' that his main work is done. Johane Masowe himself appointed all of his evangelists, but the latter have been empowered by him to choose preachers, prophets and councillors in accordance with prophetic utterances. The ceremony of ordination, like that of marriage, is simple. Those to be ordained are brought into a circle during a prayer-service while the congregation sings. The prophets present reveal the dangers which might prevent them from carrying out their duties properly, and the evangelist(s) lays hands upon them and prays that the holy spirit may come down upon them.

BURIAL

The ordained members of the Apostles, as well as the Sisters, are treated with greater ceremonial than ordinary members when they die. Three days without work are observed in the case of the former whereas only one day is observed in the case of the latter. If possible, the Apostles insist on burying their members in their own cemeteries, but in the urban areas, such as Lusaka, they have agreed to use public cemeteries.

The funeral ceremony is as follows: The Apostles first of all gather at the house of the deceased to pray for him/her, and the deceased is placed in a coffin. The evangelist tells those present that there is to be no weeping or wailing during the funeral as Johane had strictly forbidden such behaviour. He believed that such a display of grief betrayed a lack of confidence in God. As the coffin is carried out from the house, the people stand in a line singing, 'Guide us, Jehovah'. When the funeral procession has reached the cemetery, an evangelist, a preacher, and a prophet walk in front of the coffin while the people sing the hymn, 'Remain with us'. In between singing, the preacher, who stands between the evangelist and the prophet, reads from the Bible. When the procession reaches the grave, the coffin is placed on the ground and all present pray. Then the coffin is lowered into the grave and the women fill in the grave piling stones on top. The rest sing while this is taking place. Murphree (1969, 103, n.1) mentions that the Maranke technique of burying their dead differs from the traditional method of digging a 'shelf' on the side of the grave on which the corpse is placed with legs bent and bound. The same is true of the Masowe method of burial. The corpse is stretched out fully with head pointing towards the west and facing upwards. In this way, the Apostles believe that the deceased will be able to see the Lord coming from the east on the day when their bodies will be resurrected. The Apostles always clothe their dead in white.

Before leaving the grave, all sit down and the evangelist and others preach. After this, the people are told to go and wash in a river. This custom has both traditional (Bullock, 1927, 269) and biblical roots for contact with the dead is believed to incur defilement. If there is no river close by, people may wash from basins of water. It was customary to wash the whole body, but today, only the face, hands, and feet are washed. People then return to the house of the deceased once again and pray there. This is probably based on the belief that the house had to be purified also by prayer. The funeral ceremony is now complete. In traditional burial rites, beer was brewed for the ceremony and an ox or other animal was slaughtered and consumed afterwards by the mourners. The Apostles forbid any such behaviour, but tea, soft drinks and bread are supplied for those present afterwards.

From the foregoing pages it can be seen that Masowe religious ritual has been strongly influenced by biblical practice. Unlike the Maranke Apostles, the Masowe Apostles do not at present have any form of Communion Service or Pascha (Jules-Rosette, 1973, 89). Furthermore, they do not observe the Maranke practice of walking on fire (*The New Witness of the Apostles,* 8; Jules-Rosette, 1973, 89).

RELIGIOUS RITUAL AND MAGIC

Religion deals with man's apprehension of, and relationship to, certain numinous powers which remain mysteriously remote from his world and yet are believed to have a strong influence either directly or indirectly on his life and activity. Ritual is the exterior form of approach which man takes towards the supernatural Being or beings in whom he believes; it is the 'etiquette' of religion. In the case of the Masowe Apostles, religious belief and ritual are focused on Jehovah, the God of the Bible, who has chosen them as his people. Joachim Wach (1951, 41) has most appropriately observed that it is the explicit intention of believers which marks the difference between a religious and a magical act. In the case of the former, man bows down in submission and adoration; in the case of the latter, man strives to appropriate and manipulate as much power as will yield to his command. From the point of view of intention, the ritual of the Apostles is composed of religious acts, but members also believe that the power of the spirit can be attained as the result of prayerful supplication. The power of the spirit is believed to work through the cleansing waters of baptism, the singing of the Sisters and others, the persons of the prophets, the word of the Bible, and the laying on of hands for ordinations and healings. In all of these actions, however, success depends on the proper invocation of the spirit. The Apostles' understanding of the manner in which the power of the spirit works is undoubtedly strongly influenced by traditional concepts of charms and magical objects, but the conscious orientation is towards an explicit rejection of the use of all icons and other material objects during worship except the Bible. The use of water for baptism, the laying on of hands, and singing are practiced because they are mentioned in the Bible. Peel (1968, 17–18) has rightly questioned the usefulness of the expressive/instrumental distinction between religion and magic respectively in regard to African religious movements which are traditionally so this-worldly in orientation, and Yinger (1971, 77–8) has observed that certain 'magical' components are included in all forms of religious ritual. If one is to use the magic-religion bipolar typology, it seems necessary to conclude with Goode (1951, 50) that particular acts of ritual worship will always fall somewhere on the continuum which joins them. This is certainly true of the Masowe Apostles' participation in religious ritual.

CHAPTER FIVE

ORGANISATIONAL STRUCTURE

COLLECTIVE CHARISMA

Baëta (1962, 3–4) has observed in regard to the vocation of a prophet that, although the stimulus may be provided by intolerable social, political and religious conditions or a combination of these, the dream or vision itself which the prophet experiences need not necessarily be related to prevailing conditions. Peel (1968, 14) has further noted that the personal psychology of the prophet may influence the content of the new religion and may partially determine the religious responses to it. Both of the above remarks are relevant in the case of Johane Masowe. His visionary experiences were the result of a profound religious conversion which marked a distinct turning point in his life, a point from which he never turned back. They were cast within a biblical framework of apocalyptic imagery and, although containing millennial and anti-white elements, their main thrust was directed towards the fulfilment of the work of John the Baptist in regard to African peoples. Endowed with a naturally religious temperament and disposition, Johane believed that he had been chosen to perform that role.

At the same time, it must be remembered that Johane was a product of his own culture and society facing the same problems and frustrations as those of his own people in a situation of culture contact with the white Western world and conditioned by traditional thought-patterns. Under the widespread influence of the Bible and Christian teaching, what Johane experienced in a uniquely personal fashion was a call which was both relevant and meaningful to a great many Shona, and his message fell on receptive ears. As Worsley has said of the initial stages of a religious movement:

> Without the message, there can be no serious content to the communication. . . . And it cannot be *any* message: it must, firstly, speak to unsatisfied wants in the hearers, and, secondly, offer them some promise of eventual fulfilment (1957, xiii–xiv).

Johane's message supplied both of these requirements, and it did so within a religious framework. His first followers were apparently composed of young men like himself, men who were being most affected by the impact of the Western world. As a result of Christian teaching and village schools, they had begun to question many of the traditionally accepted religious beliefs. As a result of migrant labour to the urban districts, traditional social structures had begun to break down and young Shona men had become more familiar with the ways of the urban dweller. The oppressed situation of the black man was more keenly felt by these young men whose hopes had been raised by the teaching of the Christian churches, the elementary education of the village schools and mission schools, and the new opportunities which seemed to be so numerous in the urban areas. For some years, young Shona men had returned from their work in the towns, the mines, or on European farms bringing back to their villages a variety of European goods, thereby achieving a new kind of status among their own people. With the severe economic slump of the early 1930s, however, this had all changed. Great numbers of young Shona had to return to their villages because there was no work for them in the towns and urban districts. The result was increased idleness and discontent.

Many young Shona at this time felt caught between two worlds, yet belonging to none. On the one hand, they had little stake in the traditional power structure which was controlled by the elders and they had become critical and sceptical of traditional beliefs and customs. On the other hand, they had no opportunity of sharing in the white-controlled world of politics and religion. Very few Africans had been given positions of authority in the established mission churches, and the intellectual training required was far beyond the meagre educational attainments of most young Shona. The Shona-Ndebele Risings of 1896 and 1897 had demonstrated not only the futility of an armed rebellion against white rule but also the weakness of traditional religious powers. At the same time, white Christianity had demonstrated a manifest superiority which was seen to have endowed white people with manifold benefits of power, prestige and prosperity. Many young Shona were therefore seeking for some acceptable solution to their deprived situation in a manner which would (1) give them the power, prestige and authority which had been denied them in their traditional socio-religious structure, (2) avoid any military conflict with their white oppressors, and (3) supply them with the advantages of the new and more powerful Christian religion. Johane Masowe had presented them with just such a solution. This saving power was to be found in the holy spirit which would work primarily through the person of Johane Masowe himself but which would be administered to African people in general through officially appointed and recognised religious functionaries. The concept of charisma can be usefully introduced at this point.

Charisma is a sociological and not a psychological concept (Stark, 1966–72, 4:98, 36–7; Wilson, 1973, 499; Worsley, 1957, x–xv). It is essentially a social relationship and not, as Max Weber would have it (1969, 358) an attribute of individual personality or a mystical quality. The charismatic leader, of course, must be endowed with certain personal characteristics which enable him to express his message in a convincing and heightened fashion, but his appeal will only become effective as the basis for collective social action if it has been 'perceived, invested with meaning, and acted upon by significant others' (Worsley, 1957, xi). In the words of Bryan Wilson, 'On his part, he must have some grounds on which a claim to exceptional competence can rest; on theirs, there must already be an ethos propitious to the mobilisation of sentiments. But charisma expresses the balance of claim and acceptance. . . .' (Wilson, 1973, 156–7; Stark, 1966–72, 4:36–7). Max Weber (1969, 361–2, 370; Stark, 1966–72, 4:109) has observed that once the authority of the religious leader has been established and control over large numbers of followers has become necessary, a process of routinisation sets in whereby a division of functions becomes the very essence of bureaucratic organisation. He regarded this 'routinisation of charisma' as being merely artificial or sham charisma compared to that of the founder (363–4) whereas Werner Stark (4:161) regards it as being just as real and genuine as the personal charisma of the founder, although of a different kind. Stark refers to it as 'collective charisma' which he understands in terms of the gradual unfolding of the in-dwelling characteristics of the original charisma (4:112). This latter concept would appear to be particularly helpful in analysing the organisational structure of the Masowe Apostles, and this is what I shall mean whenever I refer to the Masowe charisma. The Masowe charisma had become apparent at a very early stage among those who had become Johane's inner core of disciples, and Wach has rightly observed that 'the tendency towards organisation is never absent, being apparent to a certain degree even in the "circles" ' (1967, 141).

Johane Masowe had appeared on the hill of Marimba claiming to be possessed by the holy spirit of God and, with Bible in hand, proclaiming the word of God to African peoples as their specially sent messenger. He was soon to share both of these roles with his followers. The prophets would continue to express the on-going and direct communication of the spirit of God with his people, and the pastors (i.e., evangelists and preachers) would continue to proclaim the word of God in the Bible. The prophets and the pastors, however, were to be understood in terms of their relationship to Johane Masowe himself in whom dwelt the fullness of the spirit of God and the fullness of the word of God (see pp. 47–9 above). It would be more accurate still to say that the prophets and the pastors were to embody in a more organised fashion, not the spirit and the word of Johane Masowe but rather the spirit and the word of Jehovah whom he represented. It was not the person of Johane which was of crucial significance, but rather what he stood for. The Masowe charisma rested on the receptive response to the message which he carried in himself.

PROPHETS AND 'TEACHERS'

The Masowe prophets are of of two types, the first type being referred to simply as 'prophets' and the second type as 'teachers' (see pp. 81–8 above). Both are believed to be endowed with the gifts of the spirit, the former with the gift of prophecy and the latter with the gift of tongues. Whereas the spirit communicates with the people through visions and dreams in the case of the former, in the case of the latter the spirit speaks directly to the people and 'teaches' them. 'Teachers' are, therefore, spoken of as having the spirit of teaching and they are frequently referred to as *vasvikiro,* the term which was traditionally used of the spirit mediums of *Mwari* God. The difference, however, between Johane Masowe and the 'teachers' is that whereas the former always spoke with the spirit, the latter only do so on special occasions. When the latter formally teach, they are often said to be expressing the words of Johane Masowe, but this has to be understood in terms of Johane's full possession of the spirit in which they periodically share. Like Johane himself, the 'teachers' cannot say anything which may be contrary to what is contained in the Bible.

The first type prophets have also taken over a traditional role, namely, that of the diviner-herbalist (Daneel, 1971, 144) (*nganga*), less accurately referred to as the witchdoctor. Gelfand writes of his function in traditional Shona society as follows:

> European society has no one quite like the *nganga,* an individual to whom people can turn in every kind of difficulty. He is a doctor in sickness, a priest in religious matters, a lawyer in legal issues. a policeman in the detection and prevention of crime, a possessor of magical preparations which increase crops and instil special skills and talents into his clients. He fills a great need in African society, his presence gives assurance in the whole community (1964, 55).

The diviner-herbalist, therefore, had a very wide-ranging role to play and he was consulted on every matter of any importance. He was the one to whom people turned when in need. By virtue of his special powers, he was expected to be able to diagnose the cause of every illness and to suggest the proper remedy. In most cases, illnesses of various kinds were attributed to the power of evil spirits who had gained control over their subjects as a result of some magical preparation which a witch had used against them. Johane had come to regard witches (*varoyi*) as the embodiment of evil in traditional Shona society (B44) and, even though the Witchcraft Suppression Ordinance was in force, he blamed the established white churches for their failure to condemn witches strongly enough (B60). He himself had now come to destroy witchcraft practices and he had stirred up in others the desire to reveal the presence of witches through the power of the holy spirit. The spirit first descended on the prophets early in 1933 when Johane had gathered some of his followers on the hill of Chinyamatamba in the Wedza reserve. Cyprian Nedewedzo described their work as follows:

> When the prophets started, their work was to reveal in prophecy the sins of the people. If anyone did not confess his sin, the prophets would pick him out and confront him with his sin. The word of *Baba* Johane had said that whoever had bad medicines (*mishonga yakaipa*) should bring them to be burnt. There were some, however, who did not do this. They were just trying to deceive others. The prophets would then pick them out and expose them along with their charms [*mazango* = clothwrapped charms]. . . . While the prophets were doing this work, the people came to realise that the spirit was very powerful indeed and could reveal what was hidden. They began to see that it was useless to try and conceal anything, especially that which was sinful, because the prophets would reveal it. Everyone, then, began to run off to his home to collect his bad medicines. Some brought flesh, some brought human bones, some brought human skins.

It is clear from the above that the prophets had begun to take over the role of the diviner-herbalist in the name of the holy spirit. Prophet Davison Zinenga described an incident to me in which this newly attained power to reveal what was hidden was demonstrated:

> When we returned to Makumbureka, a white man had come in connection with his cattle which had been stolen at Mahopo. All these cattle had been killed except one, and the thieves had been apprehended. I was working for Makumbure at the time, and he told the white man that I was a prophet. The pelts of the stolen cattle had been mixed up with those of other cattle, and it was very difficult to tell them apart. *Baba* Johane was with me at this time and he said to me: 'Davison, do you think that you can distinguish the stolen pelts from the others?' I answered, 'If God wills, I will see them.' So we prayed, and God showed me how to find the stolen ones. . . . The white men were astonished and they asked me how I was able to do this. I told them that it was *Baba* Johane who was enabling me to do these things.

In this passage, the prophet makes it clear that his power to reveal what was hidden had come from God as the result of prayer. At the same time, he attributed it to *Baba* Johane. The reason he could do this was because it was due to the prayer of *Baba* Johane, rather than to his own, that the outcome had been successful. Johane was the mediator through whose intercession God's power was given to his followers. This was brought out more clearly in the following incident, also related by prophet Zinenga, demonstrating the prophet's power to heal:

> When I had heard that *Baba* Johane had come, I went to him. When he had put his hands on my head, the spirit of prophecy entered into me.
>
> We walked as far as the village of Chongo in Masango, and we found that there was a girl ill there. We were asked to pray for the child, but the girl died. The relatives then said to me, 'Leave us, for you are doing no good.' I told *Baba* that we were being chased away by the relatives of the dead girl who were not believers. He just told us to go back and pray. We returned and prayed, but the child still remained dead. We went and told *Baba* but he told us to go back and pray again. This happened three times.
>
> *Baba* Johane had been seated by the fire praying alone. When I returned to the house to pray for the child, I found that she had already risen. I told *Baba* what had happened, but he reacted as if he had had nothing to do with it. We knew, however, that he had been praying all the time.

It was the power of Johane's prayer which had really been effective, and the prayer of his followers was understood to be effective only because it had been joined to his. It is to be noted in the above passage that Zinenga received the gift of prophecy after Johane had placed his hands on his head. A prophet could not receive his power to prophesy and to heal unless Johane had interceded for him beforehand. In practice, this meant that Johane himself chose those who were to become prophets, and the efficacy of their power would always depend on their loyalty and fidelity to him.

Later on, however, Johane had begun to delegate greater authority to his trustworthy evangelists, and they were empowered to appoint as official prophets those whom they believed to be genuinely possessed by the spirit. I asked evangelist Cyprian Nedewedzo how the prophets were chosen and he said:

> All those who show signs of being possessed by the spirit will be prayed for. The aspirants will then start prophesying but their prophecies will have to be verified. At first, we don't give the prophets any work to do in the church until we have proved that their prophecies are true. *Baba* Johane used to tell us to pray for certain people who wanted to receive the gift of prophecy. When we placed hands upon them and prayed for them, the spirit would come down upon them.

The work of scrutinising the utterances of prophets and of distinguishing between true and false prophets had been placed squarely in the hands of the evangelists. In the early days of the Masowe movement, prophetic utterances seem to have been rather haphazard occurrences without any form of control or scrutiny being exercised over individual prophets. Such behaviour had apparently led to serious conflicts as it had become clear that officially recognised prophets were in control of a power which was not subject to any objective norms. Prophets could not only introduce their own particular preferences into Masowe belief in the name of the spirit but they could also use their power as a weapon against those whom they disliked. A law was later introduced that the prophetic utterance of any one person in any one place could not be accepted as true unless a similar utterance had also been made by two other prophets in two other places concerning the same matter. The criteria by which prophetic utterances are evaluated today are the Bible and the tradition of the Apostles as contained in a special way among the Sisters, and it is the evangelists who are the guardians of the faith. In the words of Nedewedzo, the prophets 'must submit themselves to the pronouncements of the evangelists'.

PASTORS AND EVANGELISTS

The organisational structure of the Masowe Apostles bears a close resemblance to traditional Shona social structure. The authoritative positions of the evangelist, the head-preacher, the preacher, and the councillor correspond in many ways to those of the chief (*ishe*), the ward headman (*sadunhu*), the village headman (*sabuku*), and the councillor (*mukota* or *mukurukota*) respectively (Daneel, 1971, 32, 40). Those holding these positions, as well as the prophets, are the officialy ordained members of the Apostles and are collectively referred to as 'the elders' or 'pastors' or 'workers' (*vebati vebasa*) in contrast to the unordained members who are referred to as 'the young ones'. These are sociological categories referring to status and not to age. The elders may include some who are relatively young in age while the young ones may include those who are in their late forties or early fifties. Among the preachers and prophets, there are recognised junior and senior ranks, but in regard to leadership roles, members prefer to talk in terms of functional diversity rather than in terms of superiority/inferiority. As preachers and prophets grow older in years, they are usually appointed to the position of councillors as well. The work of the councillors is to act in an advisory capacity to the evangelists and head preachers and to act as judges in cases which are brought before them in court (*dare*). All the elders are empowered to direct prayer-services, to preach, and to lay on hands for healing, works which are strictly forbidden to the young ones. The preachers have the duty of caring for the pastoral needs of the various congregations, arranging for the proper ordering of prayer-services and listening to the problems of individual members which they then represent to the council. The evangelists are general overseers who must decide on the solutions to major problems and whose main work is to see to the continual spreading of the gospel message. Nedewedzo explained it like this:

> The evangelists are the ones who teach in the congregations. They are like the priests. They are the senior priests of this church. They are like the Apostles, like Peter. In the time of Peter, there were no bishops. They only came later. Jesus didn't have any bishops. He had his twelve Apostles. The word 'Apostles' means 'those who are sent'. They were the messengers of Jesus. The same applies to us, the evangelists. We are the messengers of Baba Johane.

During his lifetime, the two most important characteristics of Johane's work had always been those of baptising and spreading the gospel. While he had reserved the former privilege to himself alone, he had shared the latter with his evangelists. Consequently, they had become the most important and most authoritative body among his followers. They had been entrusted with the work of preserving and spreading the good news for Africa, and to them had also been entrusted the power to appoint prophets and preachers to look after the various congregations.

From the very earliest days of the Masowe movement, there has been a dialectical interplay between the prophets and the evangelists, between the spirit and the word. When Johane had first begun his work, a certain primacy had been given to the prophets in whom the spirit was manifestly at work. They were the ones who had assisted Johane more immediately by revealing the sins of those who had sought to become his followers. Furthermore, it was through the prophets that Johane had appointed his first preachers. Onias Bvuma, the first preacher appointed at the village of Nedewedzo and hence regarded as the head preacher of the whole church, described his appointment to me as follows:

> When Perpetua, the daughter of Kingston Nedewedzo, had recovered from her illness at her home in Dewedzo, *Baba* Johane left and said that he was going to Buhera. When he was leaving, we asked him how we were to remain praying. Those of us who asked him this were Leonard, Zariah, Edward Nedewedzo, Pasivero, James and myself. He told us to remain praying even though he was going away. He then said 'You asked me how

you are to continue praying? Call the prophet here for me.' The prophet's name was Aaron Kuzvinzwa. *Baba* Johane then told the prophet to pray for people who might look after the congregation while he was away. The prophet prayed, and then he came and picked out Edward Nedewedzo and myself. He said, 'These are the ones whom God has chosen to lead the congregation.' *Baba* Johane then said that we should do what God had directed.

Aaron Kuzvinzwa, in fact, had been the very first to receive the gift of prophecy and Johane had apparently wished to emphasise the fact that the preacher had been chosen by the spirit of God. At the same time, he himself had retained the right to challenge the choice, if he wanted to, due to the fact that the fullness of the spirit dwelt in himself. When Johane had begun to choose those who, as evangelists, would move about with him proclaiming the gospel, he had also given them the authority to challenge prophetic utterances which did not seem to be in accord with his own wishes. A certain primacy had hence been given to the evangelists. The prophets were acknowledged to possess a primacy of the spirit, whereas the evangelists possessed a primacy of administration and of the word. While the Apostles today regard themselves as being a church of the holy spirit, they are quite clear about the fact that the evangelists are the most important body in the church. Nedewedzo explained this to me in Pauline biblical terms by saying that people cannot receive the spirit until they have first had the gospel preached to them (see Romans 10:14–17). It has already been noted (see p. 59 above) that Johane would not follow his first preachers to use the Bible insisting that he himself was their Bible. Due to pressure, however, from his preachers who, on the one hand, had begun to feel themselves inferior to preachers of other religious bodies who were using the Bible and who, on the other hand, had come to feel the need of written material on which they could base their preaching, Johane had reluctantly agreed to their demands.

The dialectical tension between the pastors and the prophets has continued to be active among the Apostles although, as Peel has written of the Aladuras in West Africa, 'the prophet has yielded to the pastor, one whose authority derives from his ability to expound the Bible' (1968, 139). During the early years of the Masowe movement, Johane had consolidated his own position by appointing relatives to key positions, as well as those who had been personally attached to him by very close ties of loyalty and friendship. His reluctance to appoint any further evangelists since 1956 had demonstrated a certain fear and insecurity in his own position. His evangelists, however, have continued to appoint prophets and preachers to the various congregations. The norms by which they are chosen are different from those which Johane had used and are based on qualities which express an explicitly or implicitly recognised achieved status. Such qualities include seniority of membership, individual ability, upright moral conduct, religious enthusiasm, conformity to group norms, charismatic potential, social standing and familiarity with the Bible.[40]

The Masowe charisma today lacks that mysterious quality which only Johane Masowe himself was able to give to it, but the essential nature of his message for Africa has been preserved in institutional form in the evangelists and prophets. This message of salvation for African peoples continues to attract new followers as it spreads further and further afield throughout the continent of Africa. Masowe congregations are constantly reinforced in their beliefs by regular Sabbath prayer-services, and young members are encouraged to seek positions of leadership and authority by firm attachment to the Masowe way of life. Individual personalities, such as that of evangelist Cyprian Nedewedzo, keep the Masowe charisma alive by their personal enthusiasm and conviction.

DEDICATED GIRLS AND DEDICATED BOYS

Reference has already been made to the manner in which the way of life of the Sisters has become institutionalised as the praying kernel of the Masowe Apostles (see pp. 64–9 above). They have become a visible sign of what Johane stood for. From a total of 106 Sisters who were living at Marrapodi in Lusaka in 1974 (not to mention the other fifty or so who were living at Nairobi, Kenya, at the same time) the following positions had been held by their fathers:

> Evangelists: 10   Preachers: 48   Prophets: 18
> Councillors: 15   Unordained: 15

It is clear from these figures that the vast majority of Sisters have been dedicated to this way of life by those who hold or have held positions of authority as elders. Such an arrangement tends automatically to reinforce the position of the elders. Four of the daughters of the present leader of the loyalist Apostles are Sisters. In earlier times, girls were dedicated as they entered their teens or, perhaps, a little earlier. Certain widows also were allowed to become Sisters if they promised never to get married again. The three living wives of Johane Masowe are now, by his wish, living with the Sisters. In more recent times, however, baby girls are dedicated by their parents from the age of two

---

[40] For similar observation concerning leadership in indigenous African religious movements, cf. Daneel (1971, 460); Murphree (1969, 97–8). For list of evangelists see fn. 26, p. 44 above.

upwards. This means that they are socialised into this way of life right from their earliest years. Social pressure and a relatively enclosed and sheltered kind of life tends to further ensure their fidelity and perseverance. The fact that the Apostles forbid the custom of giving bride-price (*lobola*) in the case of marriage adds an extra incentive to parents to dedicate their children to the 'religious' way of life.

An incident occurred in 1963 in Lusaka concerning the Sisters which bears mention on account of the issue which was at stake (*Central African Mail,* 22.11.63). The Sisters had only been settled in Lusaka for a short time after their expulsion from Port Elizabeth in 1962. Three girls aged eighteen, eighteen and twenty-two respectively (the latter two being sisters) had been sent by their fathers from Southern Rhodesia to join the Sisters. The girls had very little desire to remain in this way of life and sought for some way of release. They eventually ran away and returned to Southern Rhodesia but they were quickly brought back by their fathers again. The incident came to the attention of the Government in Northern Rhodesia and a court case ensued. The outcome of the case was a decision that the girls should not be forced to remain as Sisters against their will. Before this incident occurred, the understanding among the Apostles had been that a girl would be accepted as a Sister with the consent of her father and would only be released on the same basis. The question of the girl's own free decision had now come to the fore once she had reached marriageable age. The new system of recruiting girls at a much younger age with the increased insistence on an even more sheltered way of life would appear to be one response of the Apostles to the problem. In 1974, between the Sisters who were living at Lusaka and those who were living at Nairobi, twenty-five were between the ages of two and three, and eighteen were between the ages of six and fourteen.

Boys are also dedicated to the special service of God among the Apostles, but, unlike the Sisters, they do not live together and they are not committed to a celibate way of life. The origin of their way of life is most probably based on the traditional Shona concept of the male 'children of God' (*vahosanna*) who were dedicated by their parents to serve at the shrine of *Mwari* God (Daneel, 1971, 86). Johane Masowe had first asked for boys to come to serve him in Bulawayo and, later on, he had sent his evangelists and prophets to Mashonaland to ask parents to allow their sons to travel to Port Elizabeth where they might work for the upkeep of Johane himself, his evangelists, and the Sisters. The years during which these boys work very closely with the elders act as years of formation and training as a result of which many of them aspire to become prophets and preachers.

FISSURE AMONG THE APOSTLES

Upon the death of Johane Masowe in 1973 there emerged a widespread split among his followers resulting from grievances which had been gathering momentum for quite some time. During his lifetime, Johane had kept very tight control over his followers through his evangelists, and no one dared question his decisions. By reserving the power of baptising to himself alone and by moving about the various congregations only at rare intervals, he had kept alive a certain mystique about his own person. It was that characteristic element of 'charisma,' in Max Weber's sense of 'a certain quality of an individual personality by virtue of which he is set apart from ordinary men and treated as endowed with supernatural, superhuman, or at least specifically exceptional powers or qualities' (*Theory*, 1969: 358–9). For many, he himself was the very embodiment of God's calling of African peoples and little conscious distinction was made between Johane himself and his message. In a sense, he *was* what he stood for. Among the early followers of Johane and those who had remained close to him during his life and travels, personal bonds of loyalty and friendship were very strong. To a later generation, however, who had been born into his following and who knew him more through their parents than through personal contact, a more clear and explicit distinction had begun to emerge between the person of Johane and his message. Young Apostles had begun to be more sceptical about the mystique attached to their founder by the older people. They had grown up in an Africa which was quite different from that of their parents, an Africa which to a large extent had become liberated from colonial rule. Even in Rhodesia itself where white rule was still dominant, expectations of approaching liberation had arisen as a result of the freedom attained in other African countries.

Ever since the beginning of Johane's illness in 1964, very few Apostles had actually seen him. He had not wanted his followers to cast their eyes upon him in such a weak and ailing condition. Many, indeed, still believed that he would never die. Because of Masowe belief that all illness was rooted in sin, Johane had apparently begun to attribute his illness to some personal failure to respond to God. Masowe records held at Nairobi suggest that Johane believed his offence to have been due to a certain lingering doubt in his mind at one stage concerning the continuation of the Sisterhood. Only after God had assured him in some way that the Sisterhood should be continued as something holy was his mind put at ease.

During his lifetime, an arrangement had been made that every congregation was to make periodic contributions to him for the upkeep of himself and the Sisters (see p. 89 above). These contributions were to be sent to persons appointed in Botswana and in Zambia who would, in turn, bring them to Johane. Between 1970 and 1973, two large buildings had been purchased and a new one specially built by the Apostles in Nairobi. The total cost exceeded £63,000. It was intended that all the Sisters as well as the Masowe headquarters should be located there. Due to the growing uncertainty over the question as to whether Johane was still alive or not, many of the unordained young ones had begun to suggest that the ordained elders were keeping the money for themselves and using it for their own benefits. Consequently sometime in 1972, some young ones from Rhodesia had brought the contributions from there direct to Johane in Tanzania at which time they had discovered that he was, in fact, grievously ill. It has become clear to them that their founder had not long to live.

It was around this time that four young ones had been expelled from the Apostles as a result of a Council held in Botswana (see pp. 38–40 above), and these four had begun to campaign actively against the ordained elders from then on. They had little difficulty in drawing to their side all those who had either been suspended or had begun to resent the rigoristic moral demands being made upon them by the elders. In particular, they attracted the sympathy of many of the boys who had been dedicated by their fathers to contributing free labour for the upkeep of the elders and the Sisters.

It ought also to be mentioned that certain ethnic antagonisms appear to have been at work. Sharp disputes concerning the question of leadership had arisen between the Shona and the Ndebele around the Bulawayo district, disputes which had also spread into Botswana. When the split eventually did occur, it is significant that the main rebel group which had its headquarters in Ndola, Zambia, was entirely Shona whereas the loyalist group in Kitwe contained a large Ndebele segment under the leadership of the Ndebele evangelist, Ernest Maposa. Although most of the evangelists whom Johane had appointed were Shona, they had begun to appoint prophets and preachers in various congregations who were not Shona in recognition of the linguistic problem which had begun to arise in countries like Zambia, Malawi, Kenya, and Zaire.

Once it had become known that Johane Masowe lay critically ill, a plan was devised by the young ones to wrest control from the hands of the elders. Johane himself was seen to be the key to success. By taking him into their custody, and by discrediting the elders with the accusation of poisoning him by the use of witchcraft medicines, they had hoped to succeed to leadership positions themselves. A similar accusation had been made at the time of the death of John Maranke. (Cf.

Daneel, 1971, 333).[41] The young ones had claimed, after the death of Johane Masowe, that Peter Chikono had received the founder's last private instructions directing him to take over the leadership of the Apostles.[42] Once Chikono had in fact taken over control of the rebel group, he had begun to appoint prophets and preachers himself from among the young ones to direct Sabbath prayer-services.

In the *New Constitution of the Rebel Apostles* which was drawn up by Peter Chikono in January 1974, it is significant that there is no mention of the evangelists or of the Sisters. Greater emphasis was placed on what the young ones had begun to refer to as the 'democratisation' of the church. As the body of Sisters had refused to join the rebel group and had acted as a mechanism for reinforcing the authority of the elders, the young ones did all they could to have them disbanded. They insisted that the purpose of their way of life had come to an end for two reasons: (1) because Johane Masowe, to whom they had been primarily dedicated, was now dead, and (2) because the goal of praying for the liberation of Africa had almost been achieved, viz., in a political sense. The Sisters, however, rejected both of these reasons for they insisted that their main commitment was to God himself and that their goal was to pray for the spiritual liberation of Africa from the powers of evil and sin.

The *New Constitution of the Loyalist Apostles,* which was ratified at the Synod held at Gandanzara in September-October 1974 placed very clear emphasis on the central roles of both the elders and the Sisters. The Supreme Council was henceforth to be composed of seventy elders, none of whom could be under fifty years of age, and this council would have the power to increase the number of evangelists. The preservation and care of the Sisters as the 'ark of the covenant' was seen to be of absolutely vital significance for the fulfilment of the work which Johane Masowe had begun. Hence, the split among the Apostles involves doctrinal issues. The loyalists believe that the question of succession through the evangelists who were appointed directly by Johane himself, as well as through the continuation of the institution of the Sisters in whom the spirit of Johane resides in a special manner, are both issues of intrinsic and essential significance for the execution of the mission which had been entrusted by God to their founder. The rebels, on the other hand, look upon the appointment of evangelists and the institution of the Sisters as developments which were not part of Johane's original mission. Underneath the doctrinal question, however, lies the question of the control of power among the Apostles,

---

[41] Concerning the use of the term 'witchcraft' see note 8, p. 19 above.
[42] For similar tactics concerning succession to position of John Maranke, cf. ibid., p. 334.

namely, whether it ought to be hierarchical or congregational in nature.

It is important to note that the rebel Apostles do not question the mission and role of Johane Masowe. Both the loyalist and rebel groups believe that Johane was sent by God as a special messenger to African peoples to bring them the message of salvation. It is this message to which the Apostles as a whole have responded. Here lies the Masowe charisma, and this charisma has continued to be present among the Apostles in spite of the split.

FIG. 10. Evangelist Cyprian Nedewedzo.

Like most African societies, the loyalist Apostles are gerontocratic. The old are accredited with greater wisdom and are accorded higher status. It has been pointed out that, in terms of Parsonian functionalism, elders have expressive functions sustaining the norms of the group and its cohesion whereas young men have instrumental functions which enable the group to relate more easily to its environment (Peel, 1968, 260). The split among the Apostles has revealed a growing tension between the old and the young, a tension which will most definitely continue to increase in independent African countries, particularly in the urban areas where the forces for change are so much more powerful than in the rural areas. The future of the loyalist Apostles will most likely depend on the extent to which they succeed in absorbing the vitality and flexibility of the young into the present power structure.

FIG. 11. Elders at Nairobi, Kenya, August 1974. *Back row, from left:* Samuel Chinyanga, Misech Elijah, Edward Monogara, Luke Matte, Jeremiah Ncube, Philip Muregerere, Michael Chiwota, Alexander Kubenda, Benet Dziwa, Robinson Sichaya Ncube, Noah Dube, Gideon Moyo, Kephas Ngomeza, Samuel Muzebe, Amon Ngomasha, Norbed Chidziwa, Amon Kaviza. *Front row, from left:* Barnabas Chipunza, Epy Kupara, Marufu Mugwira, Peter Murwisa, Elijah Maposa, Sailous Kutsanzira, Cyprian Nedewedzo, Luke Mutanguro, Philemon Magudu, Richard Mpofu, Rinosi Mugodzera, Partrick Hara.

CHAPTER VI

SOCIAL SIGNIFICANCE

THE APOSTLES AND UNIVERSALISM

Since their origin among the Manyika and Zezuru Shona of Southern Rhodesia in 1932, the Masowe Apostles have spread into eight other African countries. Nevertheless, they are still largely a Shona religious body with a strong Ndebele contingent. During the 1974 Synod held by the loyalist Apostles in Rhodesia, there were 101 heads of congregations present from Rhodesia itself as compared to eleven from Zambia, seven from Malawi, seven from Botswana, two from South Africa, one from Mozambique, and one from Kenya. Shona is still the most commonly used language during Sabbath prayer-services, and Sundkler (1964, 324; but see p. 79 above) has observed that it was once regarded by the Apostles as a sacred language. The vast majority of the evangelists appointed by Johane Masowe are also Shona. Apart from the Ndebele-Zulu evangelists, only two had come from Northern Rhodesia and two from Nyasaland.

The emphasis on the Shona language, however, did not prevent the early spread of the movement for a number of reasons. First of all, the Shona were by no means restricted to Southern Rhodesia at that time. As a result of the artificial boundaries which had been imposed by colonial rulers, large numbers of Shona were then living in Mozambique, Northern Rhodesia and Bechuanaland (Doke, 1954, 205). In the second place, migratory labour was responsible for many Shona moving to South Africa, as well as for Chewa (Nyanja) speakers from Northern Rhodesia and Nyasaland mixing with the Shona and Ndebele in Southern Rhodesia. Finally, many Shona had developed the ability so speak Ndebele which was also spoken in the Transvaal and belonged to the same cluster of the Nguni group as Zulu of South Africa and Ngoni of Nyasaland (Doke, 1954, 205).

The Masowe gospel had made its first major impact outside Mashonaland through the dynamic preaching of the Shona evangelist, Lazarus Chipanga, who had moved about in Matabeleland at the end of the 1930s. Chipanga, in fact, had been appointed by Johane as chief evangelist to the non-believing world, and a Zulu by the name of Ernest Maposa had taken second place to him. Maposa had formerly belonged to one of the Zionist churches in South Africa and he had converted many followers to Masowe belief in the Transvaal around

Pretoria and Johannesburg. When the Apostles settled in Port Elizabeth towards the end of the 1940s, Johane had appointed a Zulu by the name of Elliot Gabellah to act as one of their official leaders. They had also made a point of speaking a dialect of Zulu themselves so that they might not be recognised as Shona by the authorities. During these years, many South African men had joined the Apostles and Shona husbands had taken South African wives. Furthermore, migrant labourers from Northern Rhodesia and Nyasaland had attached themselves to their community at Korsten.

The Apostles of Johane Masowe, like those of John Maranke (Cf. *The New Witness of the Apostles,* n.d. 10) are very conscious of their mission, not just to the Shona, but to all Africans. This notion is very consistent with the early association which they had made between oppression resulting from the powers of evil and oppression resulting from white rule. The Apostles believe that all African peoples had awaited a saviour who would liberate them from their oppressors. Their saviour, however, would conquer with the weapons of heaven and not with those of earth (see p. 18 above). A text which was very dear to Johane Masowe was that from the Book of Revelations (14:6-7) which read:

> And I saw another angel flying in midheaven, and he had everlasting good news to declare as glad tidings to those who dwell on the earth, and to every nation and tribe and tongue and people, saying in a loud voice, 'Fear God and give him glory, because the hour of the judgment by him has arrived, and so worship the One who made the heaven and the earth and sea and fountains of waters'.

This text is often repeated by his followers. This form of awareness of a universal mission, however, would seem to be characteristic of religious movements whose followers 'feel frustrated in their basic hopes and thus feel no real stake in the society to which they belong. Drawing on their religious tradition, they criticise that society in the name of universal values. ... Their universalism is other-worldly' (Yinger, 1971, 474-5). Even though the Apostles today claim that their mission is not just to African peoples but to the whole world, their explicit missionary thrust is directed towards the black races. Reference is frequently made to their desire to get to Jerusalem and to India, but these references are to places which have a strong biblical symbolic value for them. As will be seen shortly (see pp. 120-30 passim below), Masowe communities are still very exclusivist and very much aware of themselves as the elect of God. Their notion of universality has to be evaluated in this context. At the same time, one should not underestimate the extent to which a growing familiarity with the Bible has expanded their explicit desire to spread the gospel to all peoples before the day of judgment comes.

THE DIALECTIC BETWEEN THE APOSTLES AND THEIR HOST SOCIETIES

The manner in which the missionary thrust of the central group of Masowe Apostles has been kept alive and periodically stirred up into flame is closely connected with the manner in which the various host societies have reacted to their presence. In the early years of Johane's preaching, he had been almost continually harassed by the authorities to such an extent that he had finally moved from Mashonaland into Matabeleland where he was not so well known. Soon, however, similar problems had arisen in Matabeleland and he had felt the strong urge to preach his gospel in Zululand. He had first of all moved down to the Transvaal where he and his followers had been harassed once again by the South African authorities, and then he had travelled to other parts of the Union trying to find a place in which to settle in peace. He had eventually found such a haven in Port Elizabeth. A process of settling and consolidation had taken place there due to lack of interference from the Government or from African chiefs. The Masowe Apostles were at that time looked upon as merely one of a large number of African religious movements, and the authorities did not trouble them as long as they continued to live in peace. It was during this period, in- deed, that a greater tolerance in their attitude towards the white Government and towards other religious bodies had begun to develop.

Johane Masowe must, undoubtedly, have come into contact with indigenous African religious movements such as the Zion Christian Church of Edward Lekganyane in the North Transvaal, the Zulu Nazareth Baptist Church of John Galilee Shembe, and the African Church of Nicholas Bhengu. His evangelist, Ernest Maposa, may well have belonged formerly to Lekganyane's church in which case he would have fed Johane with new ideas. Johane had been living quite close to James Limba (founder of the Church of Christ) in Port Elizabeth, and a certain controversy had arisen between them as to which of them was the true son of God. Limba had laid claim to the authenticity of his mission on the basis of circumcision which was required of all of his followers. Whereas circumcision, however, had been an accepted traditional custom among the Zulu people, this had not been so among the Shona. It would appear that Johane had had no answer to this on account of the explicit mention of circumcision in the Old Testament.

The process of settling and organisational consolidation which took place among the Masowe Apostles in Port Elizabeth was in clear contrast to their experience in Southern Rhodesia. In the latter, both colonial and traditional authorities had been hostile to them; in the former, their presence and activities had been tolerated. The Apostles, consequently, had even gone out of their way to co-operate with the police in Port Elizabeth whenever they could.[43] Sundkler has described a similar process of change which had been taking place among other religious bodies in South Africa at that time in the following manner:

> During the period 1913–1945, the prophet's theme was protest. . . . The interesting aspect of the development after 19(45)–48 is a tendency towards accommodation even in a culture dominated by the laws of apartheid. This accommodation can be seen in the fields of private business enterprise, education and the care of the sick. . . . The church colonies of Shembe, Nzuza, Limba, Lekganyane became not only religious centres but also headquarters for flourishing enterprise in the leader's name: village store, tea-rooms, bus station (1964, 307–8).[44]

The example of such religious movements must have played a prominent part in stimulating the Masowe Apostles to develop similar enterprises. It was not long before they had a successful furniture factory established and they controlled a large store which was called Lesca Trading Company. As was mentioned in chapter II (see p. 29 above), they had also developed their skill in basketmaking, tinsmithery, mechanical work and sewing. Due to the emphasis which the Apostles placed on the virtues of honesty, thrift, industriousness and communal sharing, they had become relatively prosperous during these years as greater accommodation and compromise was made with the wider society. The elements of protest against white rule had begun to lessen, and greater emphasis was placed on the process of internal consolidation. Bible study in particular had become a matter of prime importance, and regular classes had been established for all. A school had also been established for the children of members in which English and mathematics were taught.[45]

---

[43] When Cyril Dunn went to visit the Apostles in Port Elizabeth in 1955, he spoke with one Jack (most probably Jack Sithole) and later observed: 'There was no need for Jack to tell me that the Black Sabbatarians are an industrious and law-abiding people. It is a thing of common report in the city.' ('Black Christians', 1955:13.)

[44] See File on 'Basketmakers' at City Hall, Port Elizabeth, South Africa. Dunn observed concerning the Apostles in Korsten, Port Elizabeth: 'From the doors of their shacks they look across the lake at the bulk of a Ford assembly plant. It signifies for them, I am sure, the material ideal towards which they aspire. In ragged sheds they have metal-lathes, electric saws, drills, grinders—and a machine they have designed and built themselves for pounding maize. They have installed their own generator to give them power and light.' (Cyril Dunn, 'Black Christian', 1955:13.)

[45] Private conversation with Elliot Gabellah in Bulawayo, Rhodesia, on 21 May, 1974.

Notwithstanding the growth of a spirit of tolerance, however, accommodation and compromise towards the wider society, the Masowe Apostles continued to remain a closed community in which protection was offered against anything which might tend to lessen their basic commitment to their new way of life.[46] This has been referred to as the 'totalitarian syndrome' (Mayer, 1963, 113–26). No one was allowed to mix with outsiders or to work for them; marriage to non-believers was forbidden; and everyone was expected to work for, and to contribute towards, the welfare of the entire community. The Apostles looked upon themselves as the elect of God and they could not risk the danger of contamination from the outside world. The fact, of course, that the Masowe community was an alien group in a foreign land tended to reinforce its religious conviction of being a people set apart.

During the years in which the Apostles were settled in Korsten, Johane Masowe himself had ceased to move about evangelising with the feverish intensity which had been characteristic of his activity in earlier years. He was content to make Port Elizabeth his 'city of God' in which he would await with his followers the coming of the day of judgment. Under the influence of the Bible, he had already begun to construct a small boat, which he called 'the ark' in preparation for the approaching flood. A full decade had passed before he had made a baptismal tour of all his congregations beginning in 1959 (see p. 92 above).

It must be remembered, however, that, by this time, the fate of the Apostles, or Basketmakers, in the Union of South Africa had become very precarious. Their deportation had been impending ever since 1956 and they had begun to think seriously about finding a new 'holy city'. The increase in pressure from the South African Government—a pressure which they themselves had interpreted rather as pressure from the Southern Rhodesian Government, thereby renewing old and rather unpleasant memories—had compelled the Apostles to think in terms of travelling once again. Their growth in familiarity with the Bible had by this time caused them to think of themselves as the new African Israelites wandering through many lands as they made their way to the Promised Land. Johane Masowe was the African Moses and the body of Sisters had become transformed into the human 'ark of the covenant' in which the presence of God was mysteriously contained. It was at this time that they had begun to place special emphasis on Isaiah 35:8 which read: 'And there will certainly come to be a highway there, even a way; and the Way of Holiness it will be called. The unclean one will not pass over it.' The Apostles had begun to link this text with the plan which Cecil Rhodes had

[46] See Murphree *Essay* (1967) concerning the encapsulation of Masowe communities at Seki and at Gandanzara, pp. 35–40.

devised of establishing a line of communication on land which would extend throughout the full length of the continent of Africa 'from the Cape to Cairo'. The Apostles, therefore, as the holy ones of God, would traverse this highway, a highway which would pass through the centre of Africa. For the Apostles, the centre of Africa was clearly Nairobi which was on the equator and, since Egypt in the Bible was understood to refer to Africa, Isaiah 19:19–20 had clearly foretold where the Apostles were to build their new holy city, for it read:

> In that day, there will prove to be an altar to Jehovah in the midst of the land of Egypt, and a pillar to Jehovah beside its boundary. And it must prove to be for a sign and for a witness to Jehovah of armies in the land of Egypt; for they will cry out to Jehovah because of the oppressors, and he will send them a saviour, even a grand one, who will actually deliver them.

After the Apostles had been expelled from South Africa, then, they had begun their trek northwards aiming for Nairobi, and from there to Ethiopia ('Topia', with its symbolic reference to the freedom of African peoples) and to Jerusalem (with its symbolic reference to the descent of the new city of God).

In 1963 the Apostles had established themselves in Lusaka, Northern Rhodesia, awaiting a suitable opportunity to move to Nairobi. Johane himself had moved farther north to Tanzania in 1964 where he had remained until 1972 when his followers managed to establish themselves in Nairobi. The troubles which had arisen for the loyalist Apostles in Zambia in 1973 had also provided an added stimulus to have all the Sisters transferred to Nairobi where the new headquarters would be established.

Those who comprise the central body of the Masowe Apostles have been a migrant people for the greater part of their lives and, although they have remained among African peoples, they still regard themselves as foreigners and aliens. This fact has intensified their awareness of imitating Abraham (see Gen. 12:1–5; Acts 7:2–3) who left his own land and his own people in order to respond to the call of Jehovah. Just as Abraham became the father of a new people, so Johane Masowe has become the father of God's chosen African people. This geographical separation from their home land has emphasised for the Apostles their rejection—by conscious intent, at least—of their old beliefs, customs, and way of life. The Bible has become their new guide for living. Through it, they have taken on a new identity, an identity which involves a special mission, and a mission which has universal implications in terms of the salvation of all African peoples. In order to protect the purity and holiness of their calling as the elect of God, they see themselves as a 'people set apart' and they have taken all means possible to preserve their insulation from the wider society.

It has become quite clear in recent years, however, that exclusivism in the urban areas has become more and more difficult. The Apostles living at Marrapodi compound in Lusaka had managed to enclose themselves geographically in a village of their own, but when trouble arose between themselves and the Zambian Government in May 1973, the governor of Lusaka had said that 'they must be part and parcel of the society and not create their own empires. . . . People must realise that the Government is not going to keep people of one tribe or association in one section, and this is why we want them to integrate with the rest of the masses' (*Times of Zambia,* 16.5.73). African national leaders are particularly aware of the divisive dangers of tribalism at present as they attempt to build up a spirit of national consciousness. Notwithstanding this incident, however, the Apostles have continued to remain as an encapsulated community at Marrapodi. The situation has been somewhat different with the community at Ndola, Zambia, concerning whom the following report was made as far back as May 1964:

> At Twapia township near Ndola, five hundred Basketmakers who had been threatened with eviction have been told they can remain on certain conditions. A management board official said the Basketmakers have agreed to be scattered all over the township instead of living together as a community. They have agreed to two other conditions: that they send their sick to hospital and that they educate their children (*Central African Mail,* 11.5.64).

This incident, in fact, had arisen from a smallpox epidemic which had occurred in Zambia in 1964,[47] as a result of which 'the nine Korsten communities throughout the country' had reluctantly allowed themselves to be vaccinated (*Sunday Mail*), 24.5.64; Dobney, 1964, 9). Nevertheless, such compromises have only been made in response to pressure from the wider society and they are looked upon as legitimate only insofar as the overall security of the Apostles is concerned.

In recent years, the Apostles have become more aware of the need for education, particularly in the sub-urban areas. In Zambia, members send their children to Government schools in Lusaka, Kitwe, and Ndola. At Marrapodi, the Apostles also run a school of their own, but the Zambian Government has now insisted that children who are not Apostles must also be allowed to attend this school. In Seki township outside Salisbury, the Apostles control their own school with

[47] See Ministry of Health Annual Report, Zambia, 1964, pp. 1, 11.

the authorisation of the Department of African Education there (Murphree 1967, 22). The primary emphasis, however, still remains on the true knowledge which is to be found in the Bible. Secular learning holds a subsidiary place in order to enable the Apostles to be better equipped for Bible study, as well as to supply the type of knowledge which helps to strengthen the economic basis which is necessary for the continuation of their apostolic work and the preservation of self-sufficient communities. When Johane Masowe had first begun to preach his message of salvation for Africa, he had forbidden his followers to send their children to school. A certain sense of dis-illusionment with education in general had been experienced by many, and by the young in particular, because of its manifest failure to realise expected hopes and benefits. The response of Johane and his followers to such a situation could be seen as a rationalised one (in Max Weber's sense) enabling them to cope with an experienced sense of deprivation and frustration. Of what value was a partial and precarious formal education when opportunities for realising its potential in the concrete were continually lacking in a white-controlled society? The response of the Apostles to secular education today is still guarded, and they justify it only in terms of its ancillary relationship to religious values. Manual skills, on the other hand, are considered very important for both male and female members, and such skills are taught to their children at a very young age. Over the years, the central body of the Masowe Apostles has deepened its awareness of being the new people of God in Africa specially chosen to perform a particular task. This awareness of possessing a new identity has increased with a more thorough knowledge of the Bible. In general, the Apostles have retained an at-titude of exclusivity towards the wider society. Accommodation and change have in many ways depended on the manner in which the Apostles have been treated by the wider society. The manner of their development has been constantly conditioned by the nature of the dialectic existing between themselves and their host societies.

FUNCTIONAL ROLE OF MASOWE COMMUNITIES

The organisation of Masowe communities today may be described in terms of what Parsons has called 'sacralised polity', namely, 'the politically organised society in which the religious and the secular aspects of organisation are not differentiated at the higher collectivity levels' (1968, xxxvii). African peoples in the past have tended to inter-pret life from the context of a 'sacred' world-view in which everything was seen through religious spectacles. There was no clear line of differentiation between the different spheres of activity. When Johane

Masowe began his religious movement, he himself took the place of all that was most sacred at the traditional shrine of *Mwari* and he re-created the traditional pattern of hierarchical social structure under his own supreme authority. In Port Elizabeth, the economic substructure which was developed remained under the control of the religious authorities, a system which has continued up to this day. In this way, the subservient nature of secular activity is emphasised, and religious values and goals are kept to the fore. Religious motivation is also given to the virtues of industriousness, honesty, and thrift; and moral behaviour, along with conformity to group norms, is reinforced by religious sanctions. Emphasis is frequently placed on the danger of falling into the power of evil spirits by not living up to expected stan-dards. The recent split among the Apostles, however, has revealed the fact that the young ones are no longer willing to be so rigidly con-trolled by the elders and that religious sanctions have ceased to exer-cise a dominant influence upon them. One of the loyalist Apostles told me that the young ones had become somewhat disillusioned by the fact that no harm had come to them when they did what was wrong. They had always been told that death was the result of sin and, apparently, they had taken it literally.

In general, sermons tend to contain a strong moralistic and legalistic emphasis. Beer drinking, smoking, dancing, extra-marital sexual relations, and attendance at sports and theatres are strongly condemned, whereas attendance at Sabbath prayer-services giving financial contributions, and doing good to others are constantly en-couraged. Nedewedzo told me that controversies which have arisen in various congregations at different times have normally been concerned with one of the following four areas: (1) the traditional custom of giving bride-price, (2) beer drinking, (3) sexual misbehaviour, and (4) church collections.

Apart from the above, there is one offence which is regarded by the Apostles as being particularly serious, namely, anything that has to do with fighting, quarrelling or anger (Cf. Murphree, 1969, 216; Thomas, 1968, 233). Any form of overt hostility may be linked with witchcraft, and such an association can be a cause of great fear and anxiety. The importance of peaceful relationships between members of the com-munity is constantly emphasised and, hence, the virtue of obedience receives frequent mention: obedience of children to parents, obedience of wives to husbands, obedience of young ones to elders, and obedience of all to the laws of God. Such an emphasis, of course, tends to reinforce the authority of the elders and to preserve the *status quo*.

The Apostles do not ignore the fact that their followers are still attached in many ways to a strong belief in the powers of witchcraft. Their sermons contain frequent references to witches (*varoyi*), to the horn (*gona rouroyi*) which witches use, and to the influence of avenging spirits (*ngozi*) (Daneel, 1971, 133, 151, 156–65).[48] They counteract these evil forces, however, with the stronger power of the holy spirit which is communicated to them through the Bible, through their prophets, and by the laying on of hands during healing services. The use of medicine is rejected because of its association with traditional forms of witchcraft, and the power of prayer is emphasised instead. In this way, numerous psychosomatic illnesses and mental anxieties are assuaged, and women with problems concerning fertility or difficult pregnancies are consoled. As the women sing and the elders place their hands on the heads of the sick, the latter experience the power of the spirit in a context of group therapy with a biblical orientation.

Sabbath prayer-services perform similar 'healing' functions for the Apostles for they believe that the word of God which they hear also strengthens them in the power of the spirit. The periods which are devoted to 'collective personal prayer of praise, petition, and repentance' allow them to voice aloud certain worries and anxieties, and the frequent periods of singing serve to release accumulated tensions within a context of faith. Sabbath prayer-services occupy the Apostles during weekends so that harmful distractions are kept at a distance. They serve to reinforce the communal identity of the Apostles as a people set apart. This awareness of a new identity within a religious community which offers its members a firm sense of security is, perhaps, the most powerful attraction for Masowe Apostles. Membership of a new community restores, within a biblical framework, that mutual participation which had been so much a part of traditional African societies. Many who had been cast adrift by the breakdown of traditional values, norms, and sanctions have begun to find roots again in a stable and meaningful environment. Masowe communities offer to their members a place of refuge and a home to which they can belong; they offer them protection from the onslaughts of a wider society to which they are unaccustomed, and they supply them with the opportunity of coming to grips with new problems, particularly in a modern urban setting, at a pace which is suited to their capacity to cope with them.

It is very important to emphasise that the Masowe Apostles do not just respond to the selective needs of individual people; they respond to the total needs of whole communities. To be an Apostle is not mere-

---

[48] Concerning the Shona use of the words *varoyi* and *uroyi*, see note 8, p. 19, above.

ly a question of accepting a list of formal beliefs; it means belonging to a religious community which offers to its members a new self-identity and a new way of life, a way of life which supplies acceptable and satisfying answers to human problems on a spiritual and a material level. When Masowe women dress in their long white garments and white head-dresses, when Masowe men shave their heads and let their beards grow long, and when both men and women gather for their Sabbath prayer-services to sing aloud the 'Hosanna' song which their founder had first sung on the hill of Marimba, they are proclaiming to the world with pride their awareness of their self-identity as the people of God. Motivated by a strong other-worldly awareness of the Second Coming and the Day of Judgment and striving towards the goal of reaching the Promised Land, the Apostles cater to the existential needs of their followers in a this-worldly fashion. Praying and singing aloud offer satisfactory substitutes for traditional forms of religious worship, and accumulated tensions and anxieties are given acceptable outlets. Healing ceremonies offer similar antidotes to traditional psychosomatic problems and fears. Leadership positions are offered to those who have proved themselves, not on the basis of intellectual attainment but on the basis of religious zeal and conformity to group norms. The elderly and the sick are cared for, and children are reared in an atmosphere of love and affection. Barren women become 'mothers' through the children born to co-wives and they find companionship and acceptance in polygamous families. Due to the incapsulated setting of Masowe communities, protection and security are largely guaranteed, and the fear of theft seems to be almost non-existent.[49] Those in financial need, whether due to sickness or to other reasons, are helped from a community fund on a non-profit loan basis. This fund is used for a variety of community needs and is built up on the contributions made by individual members. When a member of a family dies, the money required to pay for the food and drink supplied to those who come to pay their respects is also taken from the community fund. All members are taught useful manual skills which enable them to support themselves and others, and simplicity of life with an emphasis on thrift results in prosperous and thriving communities. The Apostles at Marrapodi, Lusaka, are just such a community.

The visitor to the Masowe community at Marrapodi during weekdays is immediately struck by the bustle of activity which is in stark contrast to the lack of activity on the Sabbath, except at the

---

[49] For similar observation concerning Masowe community at Seki, Rhodesia, see Murphree 1967, p. 20.

masowe place of prayer. In one area, there is a line of work-shops (see fig. 3, p. 39 above) in which, or outside of which, numerous hands are at work either making furniture of various types, or forming containers for a variety of uses from sheets of tin. In numerous work-shops scattered throughout the village, similar activities are being carried on although concealed to the passer-by. Masowe men, women, and children sit outside their houses weaving baskets from bamboo canes which they themselves grow close by. The women, particularly the Sisters, can be seen knitting various types of garments or embroidering them, and many have modern machines for making clothes. Other women take care of small vegetable plots, although this is more characteristic of the rural communities which are more given to farming. Masowe men and women sell their products in the towns and cities as well as among their neighbours in the compound. Whether it be in Zambia in places like Lusaka, Kitwe or Ndola, or whether it be in Rhodesia in places like Salisbury or Bulawayo, the Apostles can be seen standing at strategic spots selling a wide variety of goods at very reasonable prices. In the more rural areas like Rusape, Masowe women have set up their stalls at the market place where they sell a variety of fruits and vegetables (see figs. 12 and 13).

FIG. 12. Apostles at market place, Rusape, Rhodesia, 1974.

FIG. 13. Apostles with wares at St. Mary's Township, Salisbury, Rhodesia, 1974.

Notwithstanding the fact that the Apostles in Zambia have recently attracted adverse attention to themselves due to the split, they pride themselves, ever since their days at Port Elizabeth, on their reputation as law-abiding communities. They speak of their founder as a 'man of peace', and the loyalist members at Marrapodi in Zambia as well as those at Seki (Murphree 1967, 19) in Rhodesia, have made arrangements with the authorities to police their own areas as they had formerly done in Port Elizabeth. The Apostles have a firm belief in the importance of establishing good relations with the Governments of the various countries in which they live. They quote the biblical text, 'Give to God the things that are God's and to Caesar the things that are Caesar's' in justification of their conduct and, although they have forbidden their followers to take any active part in party politics, they have been compelled by circumstances to familiarise themselves with the field of politics in the urban areas, thereby establishing an awareness of a clearer line of differentiation between religion and politics. At Marrapodi in Lusaka, for instance, six of the thirteen sections of the Mutambe Branch of the United National Independence Party are composed of Apostles.

Although Masowe communities believe in keeping to themselves as much as possible, they encourage friendly relationships with their neighbours. They had a good reputation among the white residents of Port Elizabeth, and Europeans in Rhodesia and Zambia (to whom they sell their wares) have expressed similar views. Bob Dobney made the following observations concerning the first years of the Apostles in Zambia:

> The sect settled down in Kalulushi and other Copperbelt towns. Their wares soon made their appearance and sold well throughout the country. In Kalulushi, members of the sect attended the Community Development Centre workshops where they taught their skills to any interested township resident. They prospered and were accepted gradually by the rest of the people—despite their unsociable habits that included not smoking, not drinking, and preferring to educate their own children rather than send them to a municipal school (1964, 8).

While basing their behaviour on biblical texts, the Apostles have clearly realised the degree to which their economic advancement depends on the establishment of favourable relationships with members of the wider societies in which they have settled.

Reference has already been made to the prohibitive attitude of the Apostles to the use of medicine (see pp. 52 and 91 above). At the same time, they have gradually begun to make more and more exceptions to the rule—always, of course, insisting on the need for purification after treatment. It has been pointed out to me both in Rhodesia and in Zambia that the Apostles tend to sneak into hospitals surreptitiously for various types of medicines which they have seen to work for others. In the case of serious accidents, they will nearly always bring the victim to a hospital. Their response to situations of illness seems to depend to a great extent on the opportunities available to them in regard to hospitals. Apostles in the rural areas tend to be less flexible in this respect than those living in the urban areas.

The educational level of Masowe followers is, in general, very low. Those living in sub-urban areas, however, are subject to a greater barrage of new ideas and opportunities, and many of the younger Apostles are seeking to further their education by attending night school. For the majority, modern techniques and ways of life are slowly absorbed within the secure setting of a traditional type religious environment in which religious values permeate all forms of activity. In such a setting, the prophets act as agents of change by giving divine approval to whatever kind of change is thought to be desirable. They also act as mechanisms for the preservation of Masowe values and norms of moral behaviour. As with the traditional diviner-herbalists who located the source of disruptive forces in the presence of witches, so the prophets focus upon the presence and activity of Satan in the community in order to reinforce group norms and to rationalise the response to those happenings which are outside the control of community members. The loyalist prophets placed strong emphasis on the inroads made by the evil spirit during the split among the Apostles. They stressed the fact that certain members had left themselves open to the attacks of the evil spirit by their objectionable moral conduct and by not obeying the elders. On the other hand, victory was reassured through the stronger power of the holy spirit who would defend those who remained faithful to his calling.

The Masowe Apostles offer to their followers a continuity with their traditional way of life and religious beliefs, but they do this within the more modern and more widely accepted biblical framework. Elements of traditional custom and belief which are considered to be no longer beneficial are strongly condemned, and those which are considered helpful are transformed into more viable substitutes. The traditional and the modern, the old and the new, continue to merge; and it is perhaps the greatest strength of the Apostles that they manage to cope with both in a manner which is both suited to, and in accordance with, the capacity of their followers to absorb. The result, however, is not merely a syncretistic blend of the traditional and the modern but rather the creation of a new African response to social change within a meaningful context which finds its justification in the word of God in the Bible.

CONCLUSION

An era has passed in the history of the Masowe Apostles, and their prophet-founder has left them to carry on the God-given task which had been entrusted to himself, the task of bringing the message of salvation to African peoples. The conscious orientation of the Apostles is focused upon Jehovah, the God of the Judaeo-Christian Bible, who has favoured African peoples by sending his spirit through and in their prophet and messenger, Johane Masowe, just as he had formerly sent his spirit through and in Jesus to the Jews and to the white races. This is the Masowe charisma which continues to attract African peoples today to the following of the Apostles. They have laid claim to a religion of their own which has appropriated the Judaeo-Christian Bible and the spirit of Jesus. They have removed the barrier of the white Christ as the saviour of the white races and have accepted the saving message of Christ as specifically directed to the black races. To say that the Apostles have replaced Christ with a 'Black Jesus', however, would be a gross oversimplification of the matter in question which would ignore the traditional religious thought patterns of the Shona peoples, as indeed of most African peoples. Johane Masowe's understanding of his new role as entrusted to him by God, as well as his followers' understanding of what he represents and symbolises for them, can only be properly appreciated when considered within the racial context of black-white relationships in colonial Africa.

Ever since the end of the nineteenth century in particular, the Shona have been subjected to the dominant influence of the white man's world in terms of religious belief and the process of secularisation. While the former was expressed through the established Christian mission churches, the latter was expressed through urbanisation, technology and the introduction of a cash economy. In the spheres of education and medicine, however, as well as in many other spheres, the religious and the secular appeared to overlap, and Christian teaching was perceived to be the herald of secularisation as well. This impression was reinforced by the close co-operation which was seen to exist between the white rulers in both religion and politics. It must be remembered that traditional African religions were all-inclusive in the sense that little clear differentiation was made between the different spheres of life in which religion permeated every aspect. Religion was perceived instrumentally with a very strong this-worldly emphasis, and religious power was believed to influence every action. Success, failure and misfortune were attributed to religious causes. As a result of the military defeat suffered by the Shona in the rebellions of 1896 and 1897, traditional religious powers were perceived to be weaker than those of the white man. Christianity, on the other hand, was perceived to possess a religious power which was felt to be capable of catering more successfully to new religious needs in a rapidly changing situation.

In the early 1930s in Southern Rhodesia, during a period of severe economic depression resulting in widespread unemployment, the religious strain was felt most keenly by the young Shona who had had most contact with the white Christian churches on the one hand, and with the influences of secularisation in the urban areas on the other hand. With little stake in the traditional power structure, and even less in the white power structures of Christianity and politics, a solution to new aspirations was sought for within the context of the new and more acceptable Christian framework. Such a solution became crystallised in the visionary experiences of Johane Masowe who appeared as the messenger of Jehovah, the God of the Christian Bible. It was he who had been specially sent as a saviour to African peoples to bring them the power of the holy spirit, the 'holy power of Jesus', which had been denied to them in the white mission churches. On account of the context of black oppression in which Johane's message was experienced and proclaimed, his preaching had taken the form of protest against the white churches for their failure to share the power of the spirit with the black man, a failure which had excluded the black man from the prosperous world of the white man. In proclaiming a message which envisaged the overthrow of the white man and the white man's world, Johane was (in Weber's sense) rationalising the religious situation. The white man's world, from which the black man had been excluded, was evil and would be destroyed; and the black man was to remain separated from all that was connected with it. It is important to note, however, that in the more extended versions of Johane's visionary experiences as recorded in 'The Good News of Johane Masowe for Africa', the central emphasis was placed on destroying the evils of the traditional Shona religious system rather than on attacking the white world. As the Masowe Apostles had begun to expand throughout Mashonaland, their main focus of attack had come to rest on witches, and their chief antagonists had been the traditional diviner-herbalists. The attack levelled by Johane and his prophets against the evils of traditional Shona religion was much more severe than had ever been conducted by the mission churches, for it took place, not within the confines of church buildings, but in direct confrontation. By emphasising the biblical source of their power, the Apostles claimed to be championing the cause of Jehovah who had sent them to root out all that was evil in their traditional beliefs and practices. They believed, however, that they were bringing Christianity to their own people in a manner which was relevant and meaningful, a manner which confronted religious needs on a truly existential basis.

The Masowe Apostles do not believe themselves to be a Christian church, i.e. a church of Christ. They are a Masowe church. However, what they proclaim is the saving power of Jesus for African peoples. They have not divinised their founder nor has he ousted Jesus. He merely performs the mediatorial and saving role for Africans which Jesus had performed for the Jews and the white man. He does this, however, within the framework of traditional thought patterns and not within the Western theological understanding of an explicit Trinitarian and Christological doctrinal belief system.

The future doctrinal development of the Apostles will depend on three things: (1) the nature of the emphasis which they continue to place on their founder now that he has died, (2) the manner in which they continue to interpret the Bible and (3) their understanding of the mystical role played by the Sisters. In the early days of his religious movement, Johane Masowe had publicly stated that he had had the intention of obtaining 'the necessary authority of the Roman Catholic Church to have a separate native church'. In the Catholic Church, there are many religious Orders whose founders are believed by their followers to have incarnated the spirit of Jesus in an unusually full and special manner. These founders, like the Christian saints who have appeared in diverse cultures at different periods of history, are not believed to have taken the unique place of Jesus Christ, but rather to have expressed the spirit of the living Christ in a manner which has responded to some specially felt religious need in a Christian society. If some analogous trend of thought is followed by the Masowe Apostles in response to their racially conditioned view of the white Christ, then their founder may be regarded by them as a saint in the manner of John the Baptist of Judaea. It may well be that, like John the Baptist, their founder will have directed them to the 'Lamb of God' (John 1:36) in a manner in which African Christianity can develop from the grass roots level of African traditional religion.

The Bible, as the word of God, has become the very centre of Masowe ritual and they regard it as their own. It is no longer just the Book of the white churches. For the Apostles, the Bible is not something dead; it is alive in such a way that it speaks to them, and they find themselves and their history contained in its pages. The whole of Masowe ritual is directed consciously towards Jehovah, the one and only living God, and the Apostles believe that he continues to speak to them through his spirit in the prophets and through his word in the Bible. While it remains true that many traditional religious beliefs remain close to the surface of the minds of many Apostles, such beliefs are being continually discouraged as members are socialised into biblical thought patterns. Over the years, the emphasis has continued to shift from the prophets to the Bible with the result that Masowe prayer-services today are largely taken up with Bible instruction.

As the praying centre of the Apostles, special emphasis is placed on the mystical role of the Sisters, and they may well become the basis for an ecclesiology of the Apostles in future doctrinal development.

The power of the spirit is specially felt in rituals of healing, but such rituals are not an intrinsic part of Sabbath observance. African people feel the need to experience the power of the spirit in a more concrete and tangible fashion than has been demonstrated in the more formal and more stereotyped mission churches and they don't distinguish clearly between spiritual, mental, and physical illnesses. In traditional African religions, while partial cures may have been sought by the use of certain medicines, total cures required a spiritual antidote. Among the Masowe Apostles, all illnesses are considered to be rooted in sin, and the power of the holy spirit is invoked for healing in a total pneumo-psychosomatic sense.

White mission churches in Africa have discovered over the years that their European presentation of Christianity has very often only touched the surface of African religious consciousness with the result that many Africans attending mission churches have continued to depend on traditional religious practices. The manner in which Christian doctrines were explained was too formally dressed in Western thought patterns, and religious ritual made little allowance for the different cultural heritages of the peoples among whom it existed. Today, expatriate missionaries are handing over the control of churches to African leaders, and the former remain on to assist the young Christian churches of Africa. In some cases, however, very little has changed, for a great many of the new African church leaders—who have, in most cases, been trained in Western-type seminaries—have merely continued to present a form of Western Christianity which is neither related to traditional religious beliefs nor rooted in the formation of vigorous Christian communities. The Masowe Apostles, on the other hand, offer to their followers the opportunity of belonging to religious communities in which religious beliefs and practices are related to their whole lives in a relevant and integral fashion. A this-worldly response to particular needs is combined with an other-worldly sense of motivation and goal, and a new way of life with clearly defined moral norms and sanctions is given legitimation in the Bible.

The Masowe Apostles are just one expression of the many creative responses which African peoples have been making to Western Christianity since the beginning of the twentieth century. It is an expression of the transition from belief in a traditional ethnic religion to one which transcends ethnic boundaries. Although the Apostles are still largely Shona in membership, they have broken through ethnic boundaries, and peoples in Malawi, Kenya, and elsewhere are responding to the message of salvation for Africa which the Apostles continue to preach in the name of their founder. Christianity has acted as a catalyst for social change throughout Africa in a context in which African societies have been disturbed and shaken by the impact of Western education, urbanisation, industrialisation, a monetary economy, and many other forms of modernisation. In many cases, Christianity has, indeed, been the cause of social change. The Masowe Apostles have given their own independent answer to what Christianity means for them.

FIG. 14. Two of the wives of Johane Masowe who are still living: Rosi Ngosi (*left*)
and Rosina Kutsanzira (*right*).

FIG. 15. Some of the Sisters living at Marrapodi, Lusaka.

APPENDIX A

(Statement made by Shoniwa to Detective Bond, C.I.D., Salisbury, interpreted by Native Detective Zakia, 1 November, 1932, S138/22.)

1. Shoniwa, alias Mtunyane, alias Johane, alias Sixpence, alias John the Baptist, no registration certificate, states: I am a Mahongwe native male adult, father Mindugwa, kraal Jonesi, chief Makoni, I am registered at Rusape. I have been called a Shangaan native by other natives but that is not my tribe.

2. I first attended the St. Faith's Mission at Rusape when a young boy. I next attended the St. Colombus Mission for a few months. About four years ago, I paid my first visit to Salisbury and was issued with my first registration certificate. I obtained employment with Messrs. H. Garmany & Co. as a leader to a waggon remaining in this employment for eight months. I afterwards was employed as a kitchen boy by a Mr Wright, who lived in Second Street, for three months. I was next employed by an Indian in Bank Street for four months. For five months, I was employed by a Dutchman at Hatfield as a leader and then was employed by Mr Cambitzi at Arbennie as a garden boy for another five months. I then obtained employment for three months with a native named Gilbert, a carpenter of Salisbury.

3. At the early part of this year, I went to Norton and was employed by a native named Jack as a shoemaker with whom I remained for two months. I left this native as I became sick. I had very severe pains in the head which caused me to lose my speech for four months. During this time, I remained in the compound of Mr Maitland's farm. I received medicine (native) from my late employer, Jack. At the time I was suffering from these headaches, I was unable to walk about.

4. During my sickness, I had a dream one day. I dreamt that I was dead. I heard a voice telling me to pray to God. When I awoke, I prayed to God and lit seven candles that I had in the hut. It was during my illness that I heard voices telling me that I was John. I had never been called that name before. I thought that I was meant to be called 'John the Baptist'. I therefore used that name. I felt that when that name was given to me that I should go and preach to the natives. I think that I was given that name, 'John the Baptist' by God.

5. Up to the time that I was sick, I studied the Bible that I had continuously and also when I was sick. The Bible I had, I bought in Salisbury from a shop in Second Street. It was in the native language. When I got better, I left the compound that I was staying in and went to a hill near Norton and remained there for forty days praying by myself. The only food I had during this time was wild honey. I prayed to heaven day and night. I did not sleep. Whilst staying on the hill, I used to hear a voice saying, 'I have blessed you. Carry on with the good work. Tell the natives to throw away their witchcraft medicines, not to commit adultery or rape'.

6. I came down from the hill and returned to the compound which I had left. I there met native Andrea. I began to preach and tell the natives in the compound that I was 'John the Baptist' sent by God. I asked Andrea to take me out to the Reserve and we proceeded to the Nyamweda Reserve. On arrival there, I preached to the natives and told them who I was. I admit telling them that they should burn their Bibles and take up the religion of their forefathers. I later robed myself in a white robe on which appeared a large red cross. This was made for me by a native named Phillimon. I also had a crucifix affixed to a wand. This I had given to me by a native named Mikale in the Nyamweda Reserve. The three other Rosaries that I wear, I bought in Salisbury from the Art Printing Works.

7. After preaching for three days in the Reserve, I went to see chief Nyamweda and asked him for permission to preach in the Reserve. This was given to me. I continued to preach until I went to a place on the Hunyani river which I made my headquarters. By this time, I had twelve disciples with me. I had a large following of natives by now. I used to take confession from either sex. I did not baptise. I did not collect monies from the natives. The only thing that I received from them was wild honey and fish.

8. I know Charles Mzengeli. He is connected with the I.C.U. I have attended his meetings in Salisbury as a spectator. I did not know him personally at that time. About a week ago, Charles Mzengeli came and visited me at the pool on the Hunyani river where I had headquarters. He did not speak to me but spoke with some of my disciples who in turn told me that Charles Mzengeli approved of my preaching and had foretold the natives that this would happen. I have not seen him since but heard that he would pay me another visit. I am not connected with the I.C.U. or any other society but my own.

9. I associate myself with the Roman Catholic Church although I have no permission of any representative of this Church to preach to natives on their behalf. It was my intention to gather natives around me and then obtain the necessary authority of the Roman Catholic Church to have a separate native church.

10. I really do believe that I have been sent from heaven to carry out religious work among the natives. I think that I am 'John the Baptist' as the voice told me so. No human being has guided me in my teachings. I am only guided by the voice that I heard when I was staying on the hill for forty days. I have heard the voice since in my dreams. The voice would come to me through a bush that was burning quite near me. When the voice had ceased, the fire would go out.

11. I no longer suffer from pains in the head.

Shoniwa, his x mark.

APPENDIX B

THE GOOD NEWS OF JOHANE MASOWE FOR AFRICA

Conception, Birth and Youth of Shoniwa
(Translation from original Shona record obtained at St. Mary's Township,
Salisbury, Rhodesia)

1. Our Lord's mother says: When I was still a young girl, I used to dream of white birds surrounding me and flapping their wings about me.

2. One day when we were at home, a man came and said to my father, 'I want you to slaughter an ox for me'. My father slaughtered the ox. All the meat was eaten on the same day and the bones were buried in a hole. After all the meat had been eaten, the man bade us farewell and left. We did not know where he went.

3. My father had two wives and the junior wife was my mother.

4. When I got married, I stayed with my husband. I became pregnant and after three months, the child began to kick in my stomach. My husband was away from home at the time as he had been arrested for not paying tax and had been taken to Rusape. When I felt the kicking, I went to my husband and explained to him what was happening. He told me that it would be all right and to go home and not to tell anyone what had happened. He emphasised that I should not tell the priests. So I went home and remained there. The pain in my stomach, however, got worse and it was not just a tickling kick.

5. One day, I got up and went into the fields. While I was walking, my stomach began to pain so I decided to return home. The pain got worse as I made my way back. Then, I saw a green cloth descending from above and a voice said to me, 'Efie, Efie, Efie'. I took hold of the cloth. The voice said to me, 'Kneel down and pray' but I did not answer. I remained silent because I was afraid. The voice said again, 'Efie, Efie, Efie, kneel down and pray'. I answered, 'Father', and the voice repeated a third time, 'Kneel down and pray'. At this point, I felt at ease and said, 'How am I to pray?' The voice replied, 'You are to pray like this: "Our Father, who is in heaven, hallowed be your name, your kingdom come, your will be done on earth as it is in heaven; Give us this day our daily *sadza* [stiff porridge] and forgive us our sins as we forgive those who sin against us. Do not lead us into temptations but deliver us from evil; because yours is the kingdom, the power and the glory for ever and ever, Amen".'

6. When I had finished praying, I stood up and all the fear had gone. The voice in the cloth said again, 'Get hold of this cloth and hold it firmly'. I took hold of the cloth and I was lifted up to a height of three feet. Then I was lowered down again. This happened three times and then the cloth went back into heaven. I remained standing and just looking upwards but the cloth did not come down again. Then I went home.

7. I told no one what had happened but I thought that it would be better to tell my husband in Rusape. When I told him the next day, he told me to go home and warned me not to tell the priests as they would kill me. My husband wrote down everything that I told him.

8. I stayed at home until the day came for delivering my baby and I gave birth to a baby boy. Whenever I shouted at him as he was crawling on the ground, he would fall down and produce strange sounds like 'Rika, rika, ka, ka, ka, ka, ka' and this happened every time I shouted at him. I went to his grandmother, Eda, and asked her why he did this. She was not able to give any explanation so we thought that it was some form of a disease.

9. When he was growing up, he would fall down whenever he was startled and would repeat the same sounds. He used to tell me that he had dreams in which people used to gather round him. He also used to make crucifixes and put them in the churches of the priests.

10. As he grew up, he began to go along with other boys to herd cattle and goats. He used to say to me, 'Mother, I shall leave here to go towards the west but I shall come back from the east'.

11. One day, I was sitting down while he and his elder brother, Shadrech, were playing. I heard Shadrech crying and when I went to find out what was wrong, I found that my son was unconscious. His father and I went to consult a *nganga* [diviner-herbalist]. The *nganga* sprinkled some medicine on him three times but each time that he did this, our son would begin to make the sounds which he used to make when he was just a baby. The *nganga* then tried to give him some porridge mixed with medicine but he continued to fall un-conscious. The *nganga* tried to find out the cause of these fainting fits by divining but eventually he admitted that he had failed. So he took up his belongings and went away. When he had gone, my son told me that there had been a man standing beside his side while the *nganga* was trying to give him some medicine. He said that it was this man who forbade him to take the medicine and that he had always stood beside him whenever he fainted.

12. When he had grown up, he said to me, 'Mother, I used to tell you that I would have to go away one day. The time has come now for me to go away'. I said, 'You are always saying that you will go away but how can you go with the disease which you have?' He just replied, 'Don't worry, mother. There is a man who keeps telling me that I shall go away'.

13. One day, while he was playing with his friends, he had a letter. When his friends saw the letter, they chased him saying, 'Where did you learn to read since you did not go to school?' Then he fainted and he remained un-conscious all that day until the following morning.

14. We sent for the priests and they came and baptised him. I asked why they wanted to baptise him as he didn't want to go to church and they answered, 'How do you think that he will rise again from the dead unless he is baptised?' While they were still there, my son became conscious and began to say, 'Rika, ka, ka, ka'. Then, he stood up.

15. I went out into the field and my son followed me. Then I saw him climbing up a mountain and rolling down stones. I asked him why he was doing this after having been dead but he didn't answer.

16. He stayed at home for a while and then he told me that the time had come for him to go away. Afterwards, I heard that there was a person in Salisbury who had been sent by God. My husband and myself went to Salisbury twice to see him but each time we missed him. We always wondered where our son had gone to. Then one day, I was very surprised when he came home with a large following of people.

17. When the priests baptised him, they gave him the name 'Peter'.

Alternative version of Conception, Birth and Youth of Shoniwa
(Account written in English by the Apostles in Nairobi, Kenya)

18. One day, before the child's birth, his mother Eve was cultivating alone in the field when she beheld an angel in white apparel holding a white basin. Her amazement was even doubled when she realised that inside the basin was a baby boy. The angel of the Lord called her by name to which she replied, 'My Lord'. Then the angel continued the address to her saying, 'Eve, receive this child for he is holy'. She took the child and to her astonishment, the angel disappeared. At that instant, she noticed a rolling rope descending out of a cloud towards her. And behold, a voice spoke to her from the cloud thrice saying, 'Eve, Eve, Eve, get hold of that rope'. She got hold of the rope which had three colours like three of the rainbow ones. The rope, stretching downwards from the cloud, lifted her several times off the ground. Upon being commanded by the voice to say the Lord's prayer, she uttered it and then went home.

19. While these wonders occurred, her husband was in prison having been arrested by mistake instead of his brother who had not paid tax. Mother Eve, therefore, journeyed to her husband and related to him the whole wonderful experience of the visions. Moreover, the most interesting thing was that upon Mother Eve's encounter with the angel of the Lord, she became pregnant. Three months had just expired when she surprisingly felt beating in her womb. Once more, she travelled to jail upon which arrival, she explained to her husband these occurrences of her pregnancy. Jack, her husband, cautioned that they should keep the matter to themselves and accordingly it was a secret between them. After nine months, she was delivered of a baby boy who became known as Shoniwa.

20. Shoniwa grew and at three years of age, he joined other children in playing. However, the strange thing was that if any of the children made noise, Shoniwa would fall to the ground in a dead faint but would revive later and resume normal conditions. Now when he was old enough to begin learning, his parents sent him to school with other boys. However, he would solitarily hide himself in a bush and when other boys left school for home, he would join them. Whenever the parents beat him for neglecting learning, Shoniwa would be in anguish and then become totally unconscious: whereupon he would later revive as was his custom; and for this reason the parents, out of fear, left him alone and so would not punish him anymore.

Signs announcing the Coming of Baba *Johane*
(Translation from oral account given in Shona by evangelist James Gore at St.
Mary's Township, Salisbury, in April 1974)

21. In the year when influenza was rampant in the country, I became ill
and remained so for three months. My father carried me to Svongosve who
had a healing spirit (*shave rairapa*). They used some snuff and medicine to cure
me and I became well. The *shave* danced while people were seated on the floor
cross-legged. The person who was possessed by this *shave* jumped about to
and fro. This was in 1928 when the locusts came.

22. At midnight, there was a roar as of thunder on earth from the east to
the west. Cattle bellowed as they looked towards the east. Cocks crowed and
dogs barked as they looked towards the east. There was noise everywhere. The
noise came from the east and moved towards the west. Many people were
awakened by the sound. Then the spirit which was in Svongosve spoke out and
said that it was the word of God which had caused this noise. The spirit said
that the word of God had fallen somewhere in the east. This is something
which I will always remember.

23. In 1931, the spirit of Svongosve said, 'The child whom I referred to is
now grown up. Everyone must now collect his cattle and kill them'. So my
father killed his cow and skinned it and took out its liver which was eaten raw.
The spirits knew that the time for their departure had come. They said, 'We,
the spirits, are going away. The word of God whom you pray to is here. This
word of God allows polygamy. It forbids the use of medicine. People must
sing songs of praise to the word of God while seated on the ground and they
must put on white garments'. When I heard this, I knew that the word of God
had come to Africans. It was being made clear that there was to be a church
for Africans and not for Europeans. That is the reason why we were forbidden
to go to European churches.

24. Then in 1932, we heard that *Baba* Johane had come. I knew immediately that he was the word of God which had been spoken of so I decided
to go to him. Everyone who had danced at the farewell party in honour of the
departing spirits was then compelled to pray to God.

25. Three of us called our families together and we went to where *Baba*
Johane was. When we arrived, he said that if we wanted to pray with him, we
would have to give him the cloths (or blankets) of our ancestral spirits (*machira
amidzimu*). We took them out of our baskets along with some beads which we
had and he burned them. Then he said, 'Let us go to Jordan'. When we got
there, some stood on one side of the river while others stood on the other
side. *Baba* Johane himself stood in the middle of the river. Then a star fell
from the heavens in the east and it lit up the river. Our families were very
happy because we had received the word of God. Then we returned to our
village.

The Calling of Baba *Johane: His Confrontation with Satan and with God*
(Translation from Shona account written by Mr Samson Mativera and dated 1
October, 1932)

26. He started by being ill, the illness of a person being punished. He was
ill for three months. At that time we were living at a farm. At night we reinforced the door with logs as we feared he might secretly leave us whilst we
were asleep. Before God had spoken to him, we had been staying in the same
house. There were three of us, *Baba* Johane, Chourombe Mazhambe and
myself, Samson Mativera. *Baba* Johane was still called 'Shoniwa' and his nickname was 'Sixpence'.

27. One day when we were fast asleep, we woke up suddenly only to find
that there was nobody where he [i.e., Shoniwa] had been sleeping. We heard
him speaking outside the hut. We wondered how he had managed to get out
since the door was still barred with the logs still in place. Outside, he was
talking with Satan. The devil said to him, 'Sixpence, heaven and earth are now
yours', and he replied, 'Depart from me, Satan'. The devil said a second time,
'Sixpence, heaven and earth are now yours', and he replied again, 'Depart
from me, Satan'. Then the devil left for a time but came back again later and
said, 'Sixpence, heaven and earth are now yours'. He replied, 'Depart from
me, Satan. Leave me alone'. Then Satan said the same thing again and
Sixpence made the same reply. Satan finally said, 'I have come to take away
my sins. I have taken my four shillings from your side'. Sixpence replied,
'Depart from me, Satan'.

28. Then we heard him knocking on the door asking us to open it for
him. When he got in, we noticed that his illness had become worse and he was
groaning with pain and gasping. The illness had now reached a different
stage. We asked, 'How did you get out?' and he replied, 'I don't know how I
got out. I just found myself outside'. Then we asked, 'To whom were you
talking?' and he replied, 'I was talking with the devil who was telling me that
he had come to get his sins from me. He removed 4/- from my left side. Then
he said that he was leaving but that he was going to pass through Sipolilo. He
said that he was going away from me and that heaven and earth were now
mine. Then I said, "Depart from me, Satan".'

29. When he entered the hut, he said that he was cold. It was in the
middle of the night. He was seriously ill. He was groaning and gasping. He
was dying. He died early in the morning just before sunrise. At sunrise, we
heard the voice of God calling out 'Sixpence, Sixpence, Sixpence' three times.
He replied, 'You are the Lord (*Tenzi*)'. The voice of God said, 'Whom are you
addressing as "Lord"?' He answered, 'Have mercy on me'. The voice again
said, 'Whom are you asking to have mercy on you?' and he replied, 'You are
the Lord'. When he was being asked all these questions, he kept on answering,
'Have mercy on me, Lord'.

30. We heard all this. We could see his corpse on the floor but his voice
was speaking with God in heaven. The voice of God then said to him, 'Sing
the song, "Have mercy on us, allelulia, alleluia"'.

31. God then asked, 'Do you know why you have been ill for so long?' He answered, 'I don't know, Lord'. God said, 'You have been ill because of the sins which you have committed against me on earth since the day you were born'. Sixpence was dead at this time. We were hearing his voice answering Jehovah from heaven. We were only hearing the voices because his corpse was lying there before us. We said to ourselves, 'One of us is speaking with Jehovah'. Then the voice of God said, 'Do you understand that you have been ill on account of your sins? I want you to come back to heaven now to do my work'. He answered, 'Have mercy on me so that I may go back to the multitude on earth'. Then the Lord said, 'Are you arguing with me? I want you to stay here and do my work'. However, the voice then added, 'Go back to the people on earth'. We who were beside the corpse were happy to hear that our friend was coming back. We thought that he had gone for ever.

32. We heard the spirit getting back into the corpse making a sound like that of air being pumped into a bicycle. Sixpence then said, 'Get hold of me'. He then went on to say, 'You people here on earth are still in the darkness of darknesses. Did you hear me talking with the Father?' We answered that we did. Then he said, 'He asked me to go to heaven to do his work but I asked him to have mercy on me so that I might return to earth to teach those who were there'.

33. He stayed alive for some time but in the evening, he died again. Before he died, he had instructed us in this way: 'When you see that I am dead, you are to take these two small boys (there were two boys with us called Paul and Luke). You are to put one at my feet and the other at my head [see Jn. 20:12]. When they are in this position, the one who is at my head will pray first like this: "God the Father, God the son, Amen". Then they are to exchange places, i.e., the one who was at my head will now take the place at my feet and vice versa. They are to continue praying in the same order and to keep changing places'. These boys spent the whole night doing as he said until he woke up from the dead again. After that, they never did it again. It was to be for that day only.

34. Early the next morning, we heard the voice of God calling again, 'Sixpence, Sixpence, Sixpence' and his spirit answered from heaven. It was only the voice that we were hearing. His corpse was still with us, lifeless and cold. The voice then said, 'Sing in this way: Have mercy on us, alleluia, alleluia'. The voice then said, 'I anoint you. I now baptise you in the name of the Father and of the son and of the holy spirit, Amen. Your name is Johane. You were there in the beginning and today you still live. Go back and tell all the people not to call you "Sixpence" any longer. They are now to call you "Baba Johane". You are to respect everybody, both young and old and you are to call them all by their titles of respect, viz., "Baba" and "Mai" ["Mr" and "Mrs" but literally "Father" and "Mother"]. Prepare my ways until the end of the world. You are to listen to and respect everybody regardless of age. All those who will believe in you will have everlasting joy. Whatever you say there on earth, I will be listening to here in heaven'. We were in that hut with Shoniwa and we heard him talking with Jehovah. It almost seemed as if we could see what was happening.

35. He was also given the Ten Commandments. Jehovah said: 'You shall have no other gods before me'. He replied, 'Lord, have mercy on us and help us to keep the Ten Commandments'. God said, 'You shall not make for yourself a graven image'. He answered, 'Lord, have mercy on us and help us to keep the Ten Commandments'. God said, 'You shall not bow down to them or serve them'. He replied, 'Lord, have mercy on us and help us to keep the Ten Commandments'. God said, 'You shall not take the name of the Lord, your God, in vain for the Lord will not hold guiltless those who take his name in vain'. He replied, 'Lord, have mercy on us and help us to keep the Ten Commandments'. God said, 'Remember to keep holy the Sabbath'. He replied, 'Lord, have mercy on us and help us to keep the Ten Commandments'. God said, 'Honour your father and your mother that your days may be long in the land which the Lord your God is giving you'. He replied, 'Lord, have mercy on us and help us to keep the Ten Commandments'. God said, 'You shall not kill'. He replied, 'Lord, have mercy on us and help us to keep the Ten Commandments'. God said, 'You shall not commit adultery'. He replied, 'Lord, have mercy on us and help us to keep the Ten Commandments'. God said, 'You shall not steal'. He replied, 'Lord, have mercy on us and help us to keep the Ten Commandments'. God said, 'You shall not bear false witness against your neighbour'. He replied, 'Lord, have mercy on us and help us to keep the Ten Commandments'. God said, 'You shall not covet your neighbour's house; you shall not covet your neighbour's wife'. He replied, 'Lord, have mercy on us and help us to keep the Ten Commandments'. God said, 'You shall not hate your neighbour'. He replied, 'Lord, have mercy on us and help us to keep the Ten Commandments'. Jehovah said then, 'Whatever you say, I will be listening to you in heaven'.

36. At this time, he had not yet gone to Marimba hill. He was told to sing:

(i) March forward, you believers:
March forward with our army;
Let the cross be your guide.

(ii) Saviour Jesus, you have come today;
You are in us and we are in you;
You are in us and we are with you.

(iii) Holy, holy, holy, holy, holy.

(iv) Virgin Mary, wonderful mother.

(v) Star of God which takes away the sins of the world,
Have mercy on us.

Shoniwa's Vision in Heaven and Consequent Confrontation with Government and Church Leaders in Southern Rhodesia
(Translation of account written in Shona by Onias Bvuma and dated 14 October, 1932)

37. There was a man called Johane who stayed at Marimba. He was a carpenter. One day while he was travelling by bicycle to Nyabira station, he became ill on the way and fell down from his bicycle. He got up and returned

home to the European farm where he was staying. He had a carpenter's shop there. When he arrived home, he was feeling very ill. There were two friends staying with him from Nyasaland [now Malawi] who were also working for the same European, and when Peter's illness had become very serious, they went to inform the European. The European came to see Peter but as he did not know what the illness was, he went home without doing anything.

38. That night, Peter dreamt that the room in which he was sleeping was full of flowers. The foreman had come to see him during the night and he found the room full of flowers and lighted candles. He then went to tell the European who came to see for himself. Once again, the European did not know what it meant and he just went back to his house.

39. The following day, the European said to some of his workers, 'Carry this man to the reserve and he can come back when he is well'. The workers were doing this when Johane died at one o'clock on the way to the reserve. The European was informed about what had happened and he went to see him at Nyamweda reserve. He then sent some workers to bury Johane at four o'clock. They put him in the grave and covered the grave with some asbestos sheets intending to fill in the grave the following day.

40. The following morning at seven o'clock, they went to the grave to fill it in but they didn't find him. He had risen. They informed the European and he said that he would inform the police. When Johane had arisen, he went to a certain hill called Marimba which is near the Hunyani river. No one saw him on the day that he rose. On the following day, they found him on the hill singing the song 'Hosanna'. They were very surprised to find him singing alone and they went to tell the European. When he arrived along with his workers, he began to ask Peter what had happened and Peter began to talk about his vision in heaven. He said:

41. When you put me in the grave, I saw a man who came from heaven. This man carried me up and we went into heaven. He took me to the first gate. I saw a man who had been sitting down and he told me that his name was Abraham. He opened the gate for me. At the second gate, there was a man called Isaac and at the third gate, a man called Jacob. While I was at this gate, I heard the sound of thunder on the inside. I also heard much complaining and I trembled through fear.

42. When I got in, I saw a great river in front of me. On the other side of the river, there was a village shining like the sun. Inside this village and also outside of it, there was an uncountable number of people. I had a very strong desire to enter this village. I walked as far as the river and there I saw a man called Peter along with two other men who said that no one could enter into this village unless he were baptised. I put one foot into the water. Then a man called Jesus arrived and he took me by the hand.

43. As he did this, a crowd of children arrived. They had been born as twins and some had been burnt to death in a fireplace while others had been suffocated in earthenware jars. All this had been done by their forefathers. They spoke to me in a deep voice asking when the world would come to an end so that they could bring their case against their fathers. When they had

been calmed down, they were given white garments and then they went away [see Rev. 6:10–11].

44. After them there came infants who had been killed by witches (*varoyi*). These included those who were just at the crawling stage, those who were just able to walk, and those who had died while still in the womb. These children were crying and asking why they had been killed. Then the angels spoke to Jesus and said that it would be better to send someone down to earth because the world was very, very evil.

45. At this point Jesus baptised Johane. Johane put his right leg into the water and when he took it out, it was white. The whole of his right side had also become white. The left side had still remained black, as black as people on earth [i.e., the peoples of Africa]. Johane asked what was the meaning of one side becoming white and the other side remaining black. He was told: 'The black side means that if holy ones arrive [in heaven], they will be sent back to earth'. Johane then said that he would go back to earth as the world was evil.

46. Then Jesus said: 'You are to go back to earth to drive away witches and to destroy all medicines (*mishonga*) because the world is about to come to an end. The different churches have failed to teach the laws that I have given them. They have done as they wished themselves'. Johane answered: 'I cannot do such an important work'. Jesus then said: 'You will speak through the power of the one who will help you. I am giving you the power of John the Baptist of Judaea who is crying out in the wilderness, "Repent and cease from your evil ways and be baptised by water and by blood because the case of those infants—the ones who are complaining to me day and night that the world should come to an end—is becoming very serious" '.

47. Jesus then said to the infants: 'I know that you want the world to come to an end, but this cannot take place before I shall have sent someone to earth to teach people. I would not be able to send them away [from heaven] because they would say, "No one ever taught us your laws" ' [see Rev. 7:2–3].

48. It was at this point that Johane was given the name 'John the Baptist'. Jesus had said all these things to him while he was in the middle of the river. Then he was baptised. After he had been baptised, he sat down under a tree. Around it, there was sand which glistened and holy grass with only one joint. The tree itself was shining as if oil had been poured on it.

49. Then an angel showed him a large village. The angel had a large crown on his head and it was like a mountain. Inside the crown, there were angels on all sides singing 'Hosanna'. Jesus then said, 'This is the song which you are to sing. The other song which you are to sing is *"Mweya Mutsvene"* (Holy Spirit)'.

50. 'I was sent into the world when the Holy Spirit was already there but people do not have strength to see or to walk. I have given you the power of John the Baptist and I will give you other witnesses to help you to do your work in the world. These others will be chosen by the holy spirit.'

51. The person who had brought me to the third gate accompanied me back and then I found myself outside of the grave. Beside me were lying a

staff, a garment which was without seam, and a little book which was sealed with glue. I took these things and climbed to the top of the hill.

52. I told all this to the European but he said that I was mad and that it was better for me to go to the reserve. So I went to Chivero's reserve and I stayed at the Hunyani river where there was a deep pool. It was there that I first saw stars falling. I used to cross the river in a canoe and go to the wilderness. I found the canoe there when I arrived.

53. People from the districts of Nyamweda and Chivero used to gather there as well as people from Salisbury. When the Europeans heard this, they sent detectives to arrest me. They brought me to Salisbury and put me in a prison cell there.

54. At midnight, an angel hit me in the face and said 'Get up and surprise them'. Then I rose up. The angel said, 'Get up and walk out' but I said, 'The door is closed'. He said, 'I have already opened it'. I opened the door and got out and sat down near the entrance to the cell. The following morning (the police had taken my staff, my book and my garment) I saw the policeman who works in the office coming to me and he said, 'How did you get out of the cell?' I answered, 'Even I myself do not know how I got out'. He went off to tell the European policeman who then came and also asked me how I had managed to get out of the cell. I told them that I didn't know how and then they put me back in the cell again.

55. For my meals, I had only locusts and honey and I never felt hungry. At 10:00 A.M. on Thursday, 9 October, 1932 [*note*: 9 October, 1932 was not a Thursday] I went into court. The magistrate said, 'Give him his garment and his staff', so they were given back to me. I stood in the witness box and they asked me who I was. I replied, 'I am John the Baptist'. But they said, 'You are Shoniwa'. I agreed and said, 'That was my name a long time ago. Now, I am John the Baptist. I have been sent as a messenger to the Africans. This is the name which is inherited by messengers whether they be Africans or Whites. I was once sent to Judaea as a white messenger but now here in Rhodesia, I am a messenger to the Africans (*nhume yevatema*). In God's language, Johane means a new beginner or the beginner of new things. I am preparing a new way amongst black people. Our fathers never learnt this way'.

56. Then they said, 'What is this new way? We know that the new way is Jesus which we were taught by the churches and the bishops and priests who have been telling us to pray, to be good people and to be baptised'. But I answered, 'If you had followed God's instructions and had done what he had sent you to do, then why would he have sent me also?' They asked me then if they had done wrong and I told them that they had. At this point, they said to themselves, 'We can't accuse this man of any crime in regard to prayer [i.e., religious matters] because we don't know what the laws of prayer are so that we might know if he has broken them or not. So let us call the bishops and priests of the Roman Catholic and Anglican Churches to question him'. The Europeans then said that they would try my case on the following day so they ordered that I be taken back to my prison cell.

57. That night, the angel came again and said, 'Wake up and surprise

people so that the name of Jehovah might be known to all the prisoners here'. The angel then took me to the prison yard where all the prisoners saw me.

58. In the morning, the police questioned me and I explained to them the same as I had done before. Then they put me in a car. I told them, however, that I wouldn't travel in a car but that I would go on foot with an escort of an African policeman.

59. When I arrived at the court house, I saw five bishops, seven priests and other heads of the churches. The Government representative was also there. They made me dress up the way they had done the previous day and then they asked me of which church I was a teacher. I answered, 'I am a teacher of the whole world. I am saying that people should stop practising witchcraft, throw away their horns of medicine (makona), pray to God and love one another. Throw away harmful medicines because the world is coming to an end'.

60. But they replied, 'We too are saying that people should be baptised and should stop doing wrong on earth'. At this, I said to them, 'Whom have you sent into the reserves and into the towns?' They answered, 'We have sent our ministers (vafundisi)'. But I told them that their ministers were friends of witches. When they asked me why I had said this, I answered, 'I was sent by God because of two babies born from the same womb on the same day. God has said, "Don't associate with witches. This is not the way that Christians should behave". In their beseechings day and night, the babies are saying, "Baba, let the world end so that we may put on trial those Christians who, even though they pray, have killed us". Why do they practise witchcraft since they speak your name? Your word is not being carried out on earth and children are being killed; some are being put in the fire while others are being suffocated. This, then, is the main reason why the children are complaining. They are saying "What crime have we committed by being born twins? Why were we killed by being put in the fire?" God then took pity on them and told them to stop complaining because he was going to start once again the work of John the Baptist, the work of preparing the way'.

61. The priests said, 'We will build a church for you so that people will come to listen to you'. But I said, 'If you want to build me a church, I want it to be such that if a child is born today on the doorstep of the church, by the time you will have gone around the church, that child will be a very old man'. The priests said, 'What kind of church can be built like that?' I answered, 'This means that I don't want a church built for me. My church is the wilderness. This means that the whole world is my church'.

62. They said, 'What will you eat in the wilderness?' I answered that I would eat honey and locusts. When they asked where the locusts would come from, I said, 'My Father told me that this year the world will be filled with locusts which I and my disciples will eat while we are preaching the gospel'.

63. The Government said that this situation required a doctor to examine me to see if I was mad. The bishop said, 'Take the clothes that he was sent dressed in and we will send them to England to King George and to the Pope. I think that all his power comes from these clothes'. When they had taken my clothes away from me, they sent me to Gatooma to doctor Philemon but he

said, 'This person is not mad at all. Just thrash him and he will stop doing what he is doing'. They beat me up, then, and blood flowed like a river. The European policeman said, 'When will you stop what you are doing?' I answered, 'I will never stop'. Then they ordered that I be taken back to Salisbury. The Europeans in Salisbury said, 'You may go back to your village now and continue with your lies'. I reached Nyahubvu and did a lot of work there.

Descent of Baba Johane on Mount Marimba

(Account written in English by church's general Secretary, Nairobi, Kenya)

64. Here on the mountain, Shoniwa was observed to be wearing a white seamless gown, holding also a rod and a small book. These three articles were miraculously found on him for nobody could tell whence they were obtained. The rod seemed to be singing 'Hosanna, Hosanna, Hosanna' in a very splendid tone of voice. However, the people perceived it as if it were a great multitude of people singing the new song. This was very extraordinary for the folks to perceive a big multitude singing whereas before their eyes they clearly saw only Father John and the rod singing. Father John opened his mouth to pour forth words of wisdom and said to the people, 'Fear God and give glory to him who made all things, the heavens, earth, sea and the fountains of waters'. These were the admonitory words which formed the theme of his first good tidings to the people and he thereby warned them to seek righteousness if they wished to survive the mighty judgments to befall the earth.

65. It happened one day that John said, 'I am going to my Father'. Now it was his habit when he went to his Father that he would lose consciousness as in a dead faint and he would appear thereby as lifeless. While in the room he said, 'Take four Bibles of different languages. Put one at my head, one at my feet, the other at my right hand and the last at my left hand.' Then after that, he died at 9:00 A.M. and awoke at 12:00 noon, and he was in a cheerful mood smiling and very exalted. Grinning he said, 'Today, my eyes have been opened for me. Although I was an illiterate, now I can read.' He began to read each Bible in turn with a face lit by great joy. There was yet another thing which surprised us greatly concerning Shoniwa. At times, he would draw the keys of heaven on a piece of paper and surprisingly later they would turn into real iron keys. This caused great amazement.

66. Immediately after John had received the word of God through the revelation of the divine presence, his diet was water only which he prepared as follows: he had a small golden cross which he put into the water, then he drunk the water as his food but threw away any extra which remained when satisfied. Later on, after a process of months, he said, 'My Father instructed me to eat rice, pumpkins and fish.' At this place during that time, fish became his major diet since rice was hard to get. Using his boat which nobody knew whence it was obtained, John went fishing in a very big pool at Nyamweda and so got his food. This pool was in the Hunyani river.

67. Now before anybody received the gift of prophecy, Father John

prophesied many things to the people. During this time, he displayed the works of the Holy Spirit which rested on him by the following means: he could understand the mind of anybody and could cast out evil spirits and of excelling impact was the power to convict the people to forsake witchcraft. He also urged the folks to stop worshipping their gods but to turn to the one living God who has eternal life. When Father John discoursed pouring out words of life, he alerted the people that there is another person who would come upon them. Moreover, this person being more powerful than them, they would not be able to control him. It happened therefore that when many people had followed him, Father John led them to a small mount called Chinyamatamba. Meanwhile, as he was on this mount with the multitude, the Holy Spirit fell or descended upon the people who thereby spoke in different languages. Father John then made it clear to the people that the person he had said would come upon them was the Holy Spirit and that he [i.e., the Holy Spirit] was now stirring in them and giving utterance of foreign languages in the priase of God.

Signs of the Divine Choice of Baba Johane

(Translation from oral account by one of the Sisters at Marrapodi, Lusaka, Zambia, in August 1974)

68. When I had come down from the hill of Marimba, I went to Nyamweda along with three other men and some girls. As I was approaching Nyamweda, evil spirits (mweya yakaipa) who were possessing people threw them down on the ground and they cried out, 'What have we done to you, the son of God? Where are we to go now as you have come on earth? We had come into people in order to find solace there.'

69. That was the first time that I had gone into any village to preach the gospel. When I arrived in Nyamweda, I was received by strangers who surrounded me and cooked for me. Some people, however, tried to poison the food and, although I knew that the food had been poisoned, I ate it and it didn't effect me.

70. At one time, I went into a house where I had been invited and the plates rose from their shelves and flew about the house three times. Then they settled back into their places unbroken.

71. One day, I asked the headman of that place for permission to hold a Jordan. A great many people had come to believe in me when they had seen that poison could not hurt me. However, they chose an evil pool for me in which there was an evil being (njuzu). They knew that many people had disappeared there. They had been swallowed up in that pool. Nevertheless, I went into it and baptised many people there and the crocodiles there did not devour me. When the people saw this wonder, they knew that I was a man of God (munhu waMwari).

APPENDIX C

The Message of God in Africa, 1932 A.D.

The Gospel of God, P.O. Box 49044, Nairobi, Kenya, East Africa. Printed by City Printing Works (K) Ltd. P.O. Box 47764, Nairobi, Kenya.

(The text below of this eight-page booklet published by the Masowe Apostles is as it appeared in English and mistakes will not be corrected.)

Fear God and give glory to him (Rev. 14:6–9).
The founder is John Shoniwa the Baptist on Mount Marimba, 1 October, 1932.
Briefly:

I was named Shoniwa by my parents when I was still young at Rusape district where I was born. While I was eighteen years old, I was revealed of God. However, before I was of this age, I frequently dreamt of myself being in heaven walking in the presence of the Ancient of Days and discussing with holy beings.

Eventually one day I was riding upon a bike, I was approached by the holy lightning of God. I fell down very unconsciousnessly, good men carried me to my room which I stayed in the compound of Norton railway station near Salisbury. I felt very ill for a period of sixty days. My soul was taken up to heaven. I passed through three gates and arrived to the third heaven where the great archangel welcomed me and we communicated to one another. On the other side I saw many children lamenting saying, 'When shall great judgment come for the reprisal of the cause of our death'. The archangel said to me, 'You are the right man to go to earth and rebuke the world before last judgment'. From there he led me to a splendid river and [told] me to put my right leg in the river and my right part was all white and my left part was as black as the complexion of a black man. He said to me you are now baptised in this river. He revealed to me that the black complexion which remains at my left part denotes that I am to return to earth in the race of Cush (the black people) and after your mission you shall call back to this holy place. The meaning of the right part being changed into white it meant that the place you are standing is holy of holies.

After that he led me to the Ancient of Days whose face was shown as none might be compared; his hair was white as snow; his head looked very old indeed but his body looked as a baby; his voice was very fearful in speech, and with great zeal.

I fell before Him with great honour and worshipped Him. He began his speech with Halleluah; he ends with Halleluah again. He blessed me and he changed my name from Shoniwa or Sixpence to John the Baptist. The name

153

John denoted 'The Grace of God' to Cush and the rest of the world. I was given power to unseal the seven seals from Adam to the last Covenant of 1932.

I was commanded to warn the world to fear God and give glory to Him, for the hour of his judgement is come, and worship Him that made the heaven, the earth, the sea and the fountain of water. There I was given three powers in one. I was instructed to teach my people to inquire the ways of righteousness through the Holy Bible.

From there, I went under a huge tree which was in a plain. I sat down under that tree I saw all the angels in heaven great and small surrounding me where I was seated; all branches of that tree were flown of many birds. They worshipped with one accord saying, 'Blessing, glory, wisdom, thankfulness, honour, power and mighty be to our God for ever and ever. Amen.'

At the east was a mount [on] which stood four Beings at the cardinal points of the mount. The first sang a song saying, 'Hossana, hossana, hossana' three chorus; the second sang 'Gloria, gloria, gloria' three chorus; the third sang, 'Halleluah, halleluah, halleluah' three chorus as well. The fourth was only saying 'Amen' after each chorus.

I began to sing as what has been sung [and] the whole multitude that surrounded me followed me in chorus. The sound was very jovious and ennoble. I stood up for my mission and that multitude stood also following me. I found myself at Norton where my body was lying in my hut. I related the story to the people who were present. The listeners testified that they heard for themselves when the voice was uttering with me in heaven.

I went on mount Marimba to begin my mission. I had with me a small book, a rod and a robe without seam which lastly were fostly [sic for 'forcefully'?] taken by the Government of British. It was on the first of October, one thousand nine hundred and thirty two years anno domini when the word of God was published upon me to spread the Good Tidings of this new oracle.

According to what I have been instructed by God, I built an ark of virgins [whom] I chose from my followers. This was a covenant of God between Him and the world. If this covenant shall last until the great dreadful day of the Lord, the believers shall be escaped out of cataclysm as it were in the days of Noah when people escaped the disaster through the saving of the ark.

The pastors, evangelists and prophets shall go all over the world spreading the good news together with the chosen covenant for ever more.

The objects of the church:

1. To believe the Coming of the Lord (Christ or Messiah)—(Mal. 3:1–2; Is. 19:19–20; 60:8; 11:6; Deut. 30; Mt. 24:37–39; Jude 1:14; Rev. 10:1–6; 14:6–9; 7:9; 19:1–9; 21:3; 22:4, 12; 7:15; 1 Enoch 77:1; 90:28–30).

2. To spread the Good Tidings to the continent of Cush (Africa) and overseas (Ps. 68:31; Zep. 3:10; Is. 61:1).

3. To lay hands on and pray for the sick (Mk. 16:18; James 5:15; Ex. 15:26; Acts 6:4).

4. The prophets work through the inspiration of the Holy Spirit (Joel 2:28; Mt. 5:17; 10:41; 22:40; 23:34; Lk. 1:70; Acts 3:18; 10:43; I Cor.

2:10–14; 2 Peter 1:20–21; Heb. 1:1; Rev. 22:7).

5. To keep the Ten Commandments and the Prophets (Lk. 16:16; Deut. 5:5–21; Mal. 4:4; Deut. 6:4–6).

6. To denounce laziness (Mt. 25:26–27; Is. 56:10; Rom. 12:11; Heb. 6:12).

7. To love one another (Lk. 10:25–37; 1 Cor. 13:1–13).

APPENDIX D

Constitution of the Gospel of God Church, Zambia Branch.

1. NAME: The name of the Church shall be 'The Gospel of God Church' (hereinafter called 'the Church').

2. OBJECTS: The aims and objects of the Church shall be:

(a) To preach the Christian Gospel both to believers and non-believers until the Second Coming of the Lord Jesus Christ;

(b) To observe the Sabbath day and to keep the Ten Commandments;

(c) To lay hands on, anoint, and pray for the sick;

(d) To bury the dead.

3. MEMBERS: Membership shall be open to any person who has repented and agrees to be bound and keep the rules and practices and/or follow the aims and objects of the Church.

4. CENTRAL COMMITTEE: There shall be a central committee consisting of the heads of every branch of the Church which will be responsible for the control and running of the Church and for any disciplinary action to be taken against members of its Church.

5. SITING: The Church shall meet at such place or places in Zambia as shall be approved of by the central committee.

6. RULES:

(a) All members shall denounce witchcraft;

(b) No member of the Church shall insult or use abusive language whether in public or in private;

(c) All members shall give freely to needy persons if they are in a position to do so;

(d) Wives shall respect their husbands, and husbands their wives, in accordance with chapter five of the book of Ephesians;

(e) No member of the Church shall smoke any tobacco whatsoever or drink any intoxicating liquor;

(f) No member of the Church shall marry without the consent of his or her parents or parent if they be alive;

(g) No member of the Church shall marry any other person other than a member of the Church;

(h) No member of the Church shall indulge in dancing or similar activities;

(i) Any member not abiding by the rules of the Constitution shall be liable to suspension by the central committee.

LIST OF FILES FROM THE NATIONAL ARCHIVES OF RHODESIA

File 1. Superintendent of the Criminal Investigation Department, Salisbury, to Staff Officer of the British South African Police, 27 October, 1932, S138/22.

File 2. Statement of Andrea in letter of Superintendent of Criminal Investigation Department, Salisbury, to Staff Officer, British South African Police, 27 October, 1932, S138/22.

File 3. Statement of Musonza in letter of Superintendent of Criminal Investigation Department, Salisbury, to Staff Officer, British South African Police, 27 October, 1932, S138/22.

File 4. Report of Native Detective Zakia in letter of Superintendent of Criminal Investigation Department, Salisbury, to Staff Officer, British South African Police, 27 October, 1932, S138/22.

File 5. Chief Native Commissioner, Salisbury, to Secretary to the Premier, 2 November, 1932, S138/22.

File 6. Criminal Record Book for Hartley, 1931–1934, S546.

File 7. Statement of Stephen Komo to Native Commissioner, Hartley, 21 December, 1932, S1032.

File 8. Native Commissioner, Hartley, to Chief Native Commissioner, Salisbury, 2 March, 1933, S1032.

File 9. Assistant Native Commissioner, Buhera, to Native Commissioner, the Range, Enkeldoorn, 11 March, 1933, S661.

File 10. Assistant Native Commissioner, Wedza, to Native Commissioner, Marandellas, 27 June, 1933, S1542/M8.

File 11. Chief Native Commissioner, Salisbury, to Native Commissioner, Marandellas, 12 July, 1933, S1542/M8.

File 12. Criminal Record Book, District of Umtali at Rusape, S289.

File 13. Criminal Record Book, District Court, Buhera, S210.

File 14. Assistant Native Commissioner, Buhera, to Native Commissioner, the Range, Enkeldoorn, 4 November, 1933, S1542/P10.

File 15. Statement of Sister Esther in letter of the Venerable Archdeacon Christelow, Director of Native Missions in Southern Rhodesia, to Chief Native Commissioner, Salisbury, 28 November, 1933, S1542/M8.

File 16. Assistant Native Commissioner, Wedza, to Native Commissioner, Marandellas, 30 November, 1933, S1542/M8.

File 17. Chief Native Commissioner, Salisbury, to Native Commissioner, Marandellas, 22 December, 1933, S1542/M8B.

File 18. Criminal Record Book, District Court, Marandellas, S1443.

File 19. Chief Native Commissioner, Salisbury, to Native Commissioner, Umtali, 7 March, 1934, S1542/M8.

File 20. Native Commissioner, Amandas, to Chief Native Commissioner,

Salisbury, 29 March, 1934, S1542/M8B.

File 21. Report of Assistant Chief Native Commissioner, to Chief Native Commissioner, Salisbury, 22 April, 1934, S1542/P10.

File 22. Assistant Chief Native Commissioner to Chief Native Commissioner, Salisbury, 23 April, 1934, S1542/P10.

File 23. Statement of Nekairo, 27 April, 1934, S1542/M8B.

File 24. Chief Native Commissioner, Salisbury, to the Honourable the Minister of Native Affairs, 28 April, 1934, S1542/P10.

File 25. Chief Native Commissioner, Salisbury, to all Native Department Stations, 10 May, 1934, S1542/M8B.

File 26. Sergeant Harold Jackson of the Criminal Investigation Department to the Superintendent, Salisbury, 3 June, 1934, S1542/M8B.

File 27. Assistant Chief Native Commissioner, Salisbury, to All Native Department Stations, 6 June, 1934, S1542/M8B.

File 28. Acting Commissioner of Police to Chief Native Commissioner, Salisbury, 11 June, 1934, S1542/P10.

File 29. Assistant Chief Native Commissioner, Salisbury, to All Native Department Stations, 20 August, 1934, S1542/M8B.

File 30. Assistant Native Commissioner, Goromonzi, to Chief Native Commissioner, Salisbury, 5 December, 1934, S318.

File 31. Statement of Andrea to Native Detective Zakia, December 1934, S1542/M8.

File 32. Native Commissioner, Salisbury, to Chief Native Commissioner, Salisbury, 16 January, 1935, S1542/M8.

REFERENCES

BOOKS AND ARTICLES

ABERLE, DAVID (1959). 'The Prophet Dance and Reactions to White Contact.' *Southwestern Journal of Anthropology* 15:74–83.
—— (1966). *The Peyote Religion Among the Navaho*. Chicago: Aldine Publishing Company.
BAETA, C. G. (1962). *Prophetism in Ghana: A Study of Some 'Spiritual' Churches*. London: Student Christian Movement Press.
BARRETT, DAVID (1968) *Schism and Renewal in Africa*. London: Oxford University Press.
—— (n.d.); MAMBO, GEORGE K.; MCLAUGHLIN, JANICE; and MCVEIGH, MALCOLM J., eds. *Kenya Churches Handbook: The Development of Kenyan Christianity 1498–1973*. Evangel Publishing House, P.O. Box 969, Kisumu, Kenya.
BECKEN, HANS J. (1965) 'The Nazareth Baptist Church.' In *Our Approach to the Independent Church Movement in South Africa*, pp. 101–14. Missiological Institute, Lutheran Theological College, P.O. Mapumulo, Natal.
—— (1972). 'A Healing Church in Zululand: "The New Church Step to Jesus Christ Zion in South Africa."' *Journal of Religion in Africa* 4:3:213–22.
BOURDILLON, M. F. C. (1973). 'Traditional Religion in Shona Society.' In *Christianity South of the Zambezi*, pp. 11–17. Edited by J. A. Dachs. Gwelo: Mambo Press.
BULLOCK, CHARLES. (1927). *The Mashona*. Cape Town: Juta & Co.
BURRIDGE, KENELM. (1960) *Mambu*. London: Methuen & Co.
—— (1969). *New Heaven, New Earth*. Oxford: Clarendon Press.
CHIRWA, PHILIP. (1974), 'Focus on "Zvinopindirana."' *Zambia Daily Mail* (Lusaka), 8 March.
COCHRANE, GLYNN. (1970), *Big Men and Cargo Cults*. London: Oxford University Press.
COLEMAN, J. A. (1968), 'Church-Sect Typology and Organisational Precariousness.' *Sociological Analysis* 29:2 (Summer): 55–66.
DANEEL, MARTINUS L. (1970), *The God of the Matopo Hills*. The Hague: Mouton & Co.
—— (1971), *Old and New in Southern Shona Independent Churches*. Vol. I: *The Background and Rise of Southern Shona Independent Churches*. The Hague, Paris: Mouton.
DACHS, J. A., (ed.) (1973), *Christianity South of the Zambezi*. Gwelo: Mambo Press.
DILLON-MALONE, CLIVE M. (1973), 'Towards an Understanding of Modern African Religious Movements.' M.Soc.Sc. thesis, University of Birmingham, England.

DOBNEY, TOM. (1964), 'Zambezi Their Jordan.' *Horizon* 6:9 (September) 4–9.

DOKE, C. M. (1954), *The Southern Bantu Languages*. London, New York, Cape Town: Oxford University Press for International African Institute.

DUNN, CYRIL.(1955), 'Black Christians build an Ark.' *Observer*, 26 June, p. 13.

FERNANDEZ, JAMES W. (1969), 'Contemporary African Religion: Confluents of Inquiry.' In *Expanding Horizons in African Studies*, pp. 27–45. Edited by G. M. Carter and A. Paden. Evanston: Northwestern University Press.

GELFAND, MICHAEL.(1959) *Shona Ritual*. Cape Town: Juta & Co.

—— (1962), *Shona Religion*. Cape Town: Juta & Co.

—— (1964), *Witch Doctor: Traditional Medicine Man in Rhodesia*. London.

—— (1973), *The Genuine Shona*. Salisbury: Mambo Press.

GOODE, WILLIAM J. (1951), *Religion Among the Primitives*. New York: Free Press.

HAYWARD, V. E. W., (ed) (1963), *African Independent Church Movements*. London: Oxford University Press.

HOEKEMA, A. A. (1972), *The Four Major Cults*. Exeter: Paternoster Press.

JULES-ROSETTE, BENNETTA. (1975), *African Apostles. Ritual and Conversion in the Church of John Maranke*. Ithaca, N.Y.: Cornell University Press.

LaBARRE, WESTON. (1938), *The Peyote Cult*. Yale University Publication in Anthropology, No. 19.

LAWRENCE, PETER. (1964), *Road Belong Cargo*. Manchester: Manchester University Press.

MAYER, PHILIP. (1963), *Urbanisation in African Social Change*. Edinburgh: University of Edinburgh, Centre of African Studies.

MEAD, MARGARET.(1956), *New Lives for Old*. New York: William Morrow & Co.

MIDDLETON, JOHN, (ed.) (1967), *Magic, Witchcraft, and Curing*. Garden City, N.Y.: Natural History Press.

MITCHELL, ROBERT C., and TURNER, HAROLD W., (eds.) (1966), *A Comprehensive Bibliography of Modern African Religious Movements*. Evanston, Ill.: Northwestern University Press.

MOONEY, JAMES. (1965), *The Ghost-Dance and the Sioux Outbreak of 1890*. Chicago: University of Chicago Press.

MURPHREE, MARSHALL W. (1967), 'The History, Doctrines, and Organisation of the Johane Masowe Vapostori', pp. 1–40. Essay written at Salisbury, Rhodesia, on Masowe communities at Seki and Gandanzara.

—— (1969), *Christianity and the Shona*. London: Athlone Press.

NIEBUHR, RICHARD H. (1929), *The Social Sources of Denominationalism*. New York: Holt, Rinehart & Winston, Inc.

O'DEA, THOMAS F. (1957), *The Mormons*. Chicago: University of Chicago Press.

OOSTHUIZEN, G. C. (1968), *Post-Christianity in Africa*. London: Hurst.

PARSONS, TALCOTT.(1968), Introduction to Max Weber. *The Sociology of Religion*, pp. xix–lxvii. Translated by Ephraim Fischoff. Boston: Beacon Press.

PEEL, J. D. Y. (1968), *Aladura: A Religious Movement Among the Yoruba*. London: Oxford University Press.

RANGER, TERENCE O. (1966), 'The Role of Ndebele and Shona Religious Authorities in the Rebellions of 1896 and 1897.' In *Zambesian Past*, pp.

94–136. Edited by Eric Stokes and Richard Brown. Manchester University Press.

—— (1967), *Revolt in Southern Rhodesia 1896–97*. London: Heinemann Educational Books.

—— (1970), *The African Voice in Southern Rhodesia*. London: Heinemann.

REDEKOP, CALVIN. (1974), 'A New Look at Sect Development.' *Journal for the Scientific Study of Religion* 13 (September): 345–52.

'Sect Widows Start Zambia's "Holy War." ' (1974), *Drum,* June, pp. 12–16.

SHEPPERSON, G., and PRICE, T. (1958), *Independent African: John Chilembwe and the Nyasaland Rising of 1915*. Edinburgh. Edinburgh University Press.

STARK, WERNER. (1966–72), *The Sociology of Religion: A Study of Christendom*. 5 vols. New York: Fordham University Press.

STINCHCOMBE, ARTHUR. (1968), *Constructing Social Theories*. New York: Harcourt, Brace & World, Inc.

STOKES, ERIC, and BROWN, RICHARD, (eds.) (1966), *The Zambesian Past*. Manchester: Manchester University Press.

SUNDKLER, BENGT. (1961), 'The Concept of Christianity in the African Independent Churches.' *African Studies* 20:4 203–13.

—— (1964), *Bantu Prophets in South Africa*. New rev. ed. London: Oxford University Press.

TALMON, YONINA. (1966), 'Millenarian Movements.' *European Journal of Sociology* 7: 159–200.

The New Witness of the Apostles. (n.d.) Translated by Peter Nyamwena. Church of the Apostles, P.O. Box 1013, Salisbury, Rhodesia, n.p.

THOMAS, NORMAN E. (1968), 'Christianity, Politics and the Manyika.' Ph.D. dissertation, University of Boston.

THRUPP, SYLVIA, (ed.) (1962), *Millennial Dreams in Action*. The Hague: Mouton & Co.

TROELTSCH, ERNST. (1931) *The Social Teaching of the Christian Churches*. 2 vols. Translated by Olive Wyon. London: Allen & Unwin.

TURNER, HAROLD W. (1967a), *African Independent Church*. 2 vols. Oxford: Clarendon Press.

—— (1967b), 'A Typology for African Religious Movements.' *Journal of Religion in Africa*. 1 fasc. I: 1–34.

—— (1968, 1970), ed. 'Bibliography of Modern African Religious Movements.' *Journal of Religion in Africa*. 1 fasc. 3: 173–211; and 3: 161–208.

—— (1971), 'A New Field in the History of Religions.' *Religion: A Journal of Religion and Religions*. 1:1: 1–10.

WACH, JOACHIM. (1951) *Types of Religious Experience, Christian and Non-Christian*. Chicago: University of Chicago Press.

—— (1967), *Sociology of Religion*. Chicago: University of Chicago Press.

WALLACE, ANTHONY F. (1956), 'Revitalization Movements.' *American Anthropologist*. 58 (April): 264–81.

WEBER, MAX. (1968), *The Sociology of Religion*. Translated by Ephraim Fischoff. Boston: Beacon Press.

—— (1969), *The Theory of Social and Economic Organization*. New York: Oxford University Press.

WILSON, BRYAN R. (1961), *Sects and Society*. London: William Heinemann, Ltd.

—— (ed.) (1967a), *Patterns of Sectarianism: Organization and Ideology in Social and Religious Movements*. London: William Heinemann, Ltd.

—— (1967b), 'The Migrating Sects.' *British Journal of Sociology*. 18 (September): 303–17.

—— (1973), *Magic and the Millennium*. London: Heinemann.

WORSLEY, PETER. (1957), *The Trumpet Shall Sound*. London: MacGibbon & Kee.

YINGER, MILTON J. (1971), *The Scientific Study of Religion*. New York: Macmillan Company.

NEWSPAPERS

South African

Daily News, Durban
Eastern Province Herald, Port Elizabeth
Evening Post, Port Elizabeth
Natal Mercury, Durban
Rand Daily Mail, Johannesburg
Sunday Tribune, Durban

Rhodesian

Chronicle, Bulawayo
Daily News, Salisbury
Rhodesia Herald, Salisbury
Sunday Mail, Salisbury
Sunday News, Bulawayo

Zambian

Central African Post, Lusaka
Times of Zambia, Ndola
Zambian Daily Mail, Lusaka

MASOWE APOSTLES CONSTITUTIONS

1. Constitution of the Masowe Apostles as Registered in Zambia prior to the Split in 1973 (Appendix D).

2. The New Constitution of the Loyalist Group of the Masowe Apostles approved at the Synod held at Gandanzara, Rhodesia, in 1974.

3. The New Constitution of the Rebel Group of the Masowe Apostles drafted in English on 22 January, 1974, in Zambia.

(2 and 3 included in author's doctoral thesis, Fordham University, New York, February, 1976).

INDEX